History T

D0494957

956.101

Ian Lyster was born in 1937 in London and educated in Istanbul, where his father and grandmother had earlier lived, as well as in the UK. After studying at the London College of Printing he worked for a number of printing companies and later set up his own book distribution company.

AMONG THE OTTOMANS

0050134876

Diaries from Turkey in World War I

EDITED BY IAN LYSTER

LONDON · NEW YORK

Published in 2011 by I.B.Tauris & Co Ltd
6 Salem Road, London W2 4BU
175 Fifth Avenue, New York NY 10010
www.ibtauris.com

Distributed in the United States and Canada Exclusively by Palgrave Macmillan
175 Fifth Avenue, New York NY 10010

ISBN: 978 1 84885 521 2

A full CIP record for this book is available from the British Library
A full CIP record is available from the Library of Congress

Library of Congress Catalog Card Number: available

Typeset in Garamond by Park Graphics, Ormskirk, U.K.
Printed and bound in Great Britain by CPI Antony Rowe, Chippenham

CONTENTS

Part One: The Diaries of Mrs Marie Lyster (1865-1965)

Part Two: The Diaries of Captain Henry Newbolt Lyster (1888-1980)

ACKNOWLEDGMENTS

The editing of and researching for this book has taken up a great deal of my time, and I had to wait until retirement to be able to allocate that much of this valuable commodity to it. Much of that time involved monopolising the dining-room table for long periods. In hindsight I can now apologise to my wife Jill, and thank her for her support during the project.

Foremost among others who have helped is of course my brother Alan who had more in the way of old family photographs and memories of his childhood in Constantinople in the 1920s and 1930s.

I was recently given a birthday present by Jennie and Richard Lovegrove, of a subscription to that wonderful magazine on Turkey and all things Turkish, *Cornucopia*, and in the first issue I received was an article on the city of Edirne. I then contacted the editor John Scott, suggesting that an article on my father's time there just after WWI might be of interest to his readers. He agreed, but also suggested that the whole of this diary, and that of my grandmother, were worthy of expansion into a book, and this set me onto the long and difficult trail to find a publisher who agreed with him.

Once on this trail and following several frustrating experiences, I must offer thanks to several people in Ormskirk who helped me with their knowledge. In particular, Ken Lees, a local PC. whose interest in WWI is wide-ranging and contagious; also Noyan Dereli, whom I met at a local U3A (University of the 3rd Age) meeting. His knowledge of Turkish history must be unique in this area.

Many books have helped me, but the ones I have used the most for my references are; *Ionian Vision* by Michael Llewellyn Smith (London: Allen Lane, 1973) – I note in *his* acknowledgements that my name and that of my father are both mentioned!

Also *Eden to Armageddon* by Roger Ford (London: Weidenfeld

& Nicolson, 2009); Alan Moorehead's *Gallipoli* (New York: Harper Brothers, 1956); Giles Milton's *Paradise Lost* (London: Sceptre, 2008); and an anthology *Chronology of the 20th Century* by Philip Waller and John Rowell, (Oxford: Helicon, 1995). Certain references listed on Wikipedia have also proved useful.

Thanks are also due to Dick Sullivan, with whom I was at Douai School in the 1950s. We now meet at annual reunions, and I was surprised to learn from him that his grandfather, Michael Sullivan (1863-1911), had been Company Secretary to the Imperial Ottoman Bank at the time both my father and grandfather worked for it. In fact it may have been he who was responsible for sending my grandfather to Constantinople as Chief Cashier to their branch in the city. Dick has sent me information upon which the book's section on the Ottoman Bank is largely based. We only recently made this connection – that our grandfathers probably knew each other, and worked together.

Finally my gratitude to Gerard Swarbrick who is well-known locally for his carefully researched and colourful maps of local areas. He has kindly drawn the line maps which will help the reader place some of the towns and villages mentioned in the diaries which follow.

Ian Lyster, Ormskirk, Lancashire

LIST OF ILLUSTRATIONS

1. Page of diary (reduced). There are three volumes, all different sizes. This page appears in the book on p34.

2. A letter written by my grandmother dated July 15th; unfortunately no year shown. It is the style and writing of a young girl (compare the writing to the mature hand in Illus.1). She signs it 'Anino', so presumably still considers herself (correctly) to be Italian despite her perfect English and her attendance at an English school (that of 'The Misses Walsh')

3. My grandmother's *'vesika'* as mentioned on p.1. Turkey used the Arabic script until Kemal Ataturk changed it in the 1930s. The heading read 'Residence Permit for Foreigners' and is numbered 145510. Her nationality is given as 'English'. She would have been 50 in 1915.

4. My father, taken in Adrinople, c.1918. The endorsement clearly shows 'British Military Representative, Adrinople'.

5. My uncle Freddie, my father and grandfather (looking very proud of his two sons). Presumably taken in Salonika, c.1916.

6. A photo taken of Constantinople inhabitants removing their goods from their typical wooden houses due to an approaching fire (see pp. 53 and 54). The girl on the wall on the right appears to be distressed. (IWM).

7. A group of Greek Irregular soldiers (or *'comitajis'*), typical of the ones my father worked with (IWM).

8. An aerial photograph showing the burning of Salonika – see p.116. (IWM).

PREFACE

I would suggest that most people 'of a certain age' have wondered why they did not ask a parent or grandparent more questions as to their upbringing and childhood. This suggestion becomes more relevant in the situation I find myself in, trying and certainly sometimes failing to fill in the gaps in our family history. I can only apologise if certain information is missing, due to the fact that I failed to ask the right questions of family members, at the right times when they were alive, or even more unforgivably, did not pay enough attention when told, and have since forgotten.

The Introduction which follows thus purports to inform the reader, as to why this branch of the Lyster family came to be in Turkey. Also to try and explain in relatively simple terms why and how the Ottoman Bank, which was so important to my family's history, took over most of the financial arrangements in the Ottoman Empire – these parts are relatively easy to research and set down.

What is more difficult to explain, are the much more complex issues of why in 1914 the Ottoman Empire chose to ally itself with the 'Central Powers' of Germany, Austro-Hungary, the Bulgarians and others in 1914, rather than the Anglo/French Entente (with the Italians), and then why, after the cessation of hostilities and the ensuing Armistice, the Greeks decided to invade Asia Minor in 1919 and 1920 to try to enforce their long-held ambition of a 'Greater Greece' with its capital restored to the city of Constantine – Constantinople, which had been lost to conquest by the Seljuk Turks in 1453.

THE LYSTER FAMILY IN TURKEY

My grandmother was Maria (aka.Marie) d'Anino (1865–1965), I think the only child of Ina d'Anino, herself the widow of Signor J.d'Anino, a dragoman with the Italian Embassy in Constantinople. This title of 'dragoman' is usually defined as an interpreter, but if possessing sufficient intelligence, a dragoman could also prove to be a very useful negotiator and exert considerable influence. I do not know of course which category my great-grandfather would have fallen into, or what age my grandmother was when he died, but she must have been quite young.

In 1871, her mother, the widowed Mme.d'Anino, married the English harbourmaster to the very important port of Constantinople, Captain Henry Newbolt (1808–89). Newbolt was then a well-known figure in the Middle East having been the Naval Adviser to Mehmet (or Mohammed) Ali, the Viceroy of Egypt. On the death of the latter, the captain moved to Constantinople as the surveyor to Lloyds Underwriters, later being appointed harbourmaster.

He was the fifth son of Sir John Newbolt MD, and Catherine (née Dennis) of Wokingham. He was also the great-uncle of the poet Sir Henry Newbolt (1882–1938). He had been earlier married to a Miss Sophy Hall; the marriage produced two daughters, the younger of whom was married to Sir Frederick Smythe, Comptroller General to the Imperial Ottoman Bank. Newbolt was widowed in 1869, so he would have been 63 at the time of his second marriage, and my grandmother Maria became his stepdaughter aged just six.

These two widowed people had very different backgrounds and it is difficult to understand how they might have met, for socially they would have been at quite different levels at a time when these matters were very important, but meet and marry they did, so my grandmother moved from the relative obscurity of being the daughter of a minor Italian official, to a much more socially important role as the step-daughter of the local harbourmaster, and she then began to be brought up as an English girl – see the letter in English to her parents – Illustration ii.

My grandfather Alfred James Lyster (1865–1949) was the fifth son of Lt. Col. Septimus Lyster and was sent to Constantinople as Chief Cashier to the Imperial Ottoman Bank there. Mixing with the British community, he met Maria d'Anino and they married in 1887, at the very young age – for those times – of 22.

There were four children of the marriage; my father the eldest, was named Henry Newbolt in honour of his step-grandfather, then my aunt Edythe Marie Valerie (1893–1994) generally known at 'Tizza' – see the pages of her mother's diary following; a second boy James Leslie died in infancy, and then finally my uncle Frederick John (1897–1979). The three surviving children had all been born in Constantinople and had returned to England for education before WWI, and then my grandfather must have been recalled to the UK at some time just before the outbreak of war in 1914, his wife, with Mrs Newbolt, his mother-in-law, were to follow. However, at some time, the old lady had a fall, breaking a leg (or perhaps a hip), and was unable to travel meaning that mother and daughter remained in the city for the duration. This is one of the main regrets I have in not having questioned the relevant people more closely, as these references should be clearer.

Now, classed in Turkey as 'belligerents', Mrs Lyster and Mrs Newbolt somehow acquired US nationality which enabled them to stay on in Constantinople as citizens of a neutral state, but when the USA entered the war in 1917, they again became 'belligerents' and their protection was transferred to another neutral state – this time Holland.

The first part of the pages of my grandmother's diary which follow were started in February 1916 and continue in three hand-written volumes (see Illustration i) until the end of the war in November 1918. They stop very abruptly, and I have no knowledge as to when the elderly Mrs Newbolt died or when my grandmother came back to England, presumably then alone, to re-join her husband and those children still in Britain. My grandfather probably carried on working for the Ottoman Bank until he retired.

I first remember meeting my grandparents living in retirement in Ealing. West London, during WWII. (I was born in 1937). My grandfather died in 1949, and then my grandmother went on to live with her now, also-widowed daughter, 'Tizza' in Surbiton, dying, aged 100 in 1965.

My elder brother Alan, contacted the archives and website of the Ottoman Bank, now merged with the Turkish Garanti Bank to try to check if and when our grandfather went back to work for them, but although the records are voluminous, they refer more to financial matters, and the main archive department in Istanbul, was unable to help.

These WWI diaries have been heavily edited by me, for some of the narrative could be considered tedious to the non-family reader. Naturally enough my grandmother was more concerned with the every-day matters of finding enough to eat and keeping both herself and her mother healthy, than with writing something which might be published a century later. It must have been difficult for her to live and manage a home without a husband, with an elderly invalid mother, and also classed as 'belligerents'. She tries hard to 'keep up appearances', wholly aware of her status as a 'lady'. She had no experience of financial matters – however, she learnt very quickly. She suggests that her diary is her best friend as she can off-load her concerns therein, but there is also much comment on the political and sociological events going on all around her as the war progressed, so it is these matters on which I have concentrated hoping they would be of more interest to a reader in the 21st century.

What strikes me most of all in these diaries, is the tolerance of the Turkish authorities towards the many belligerents who still lived in the city despite their use of valuable food and facilities. There is occasional talk of evacuation, but nothing comes of it – these people seemed to be able to move around with no restrictions. Perhaps this was due to those edicts of the Holy Koran which preach tolerance and hospitality towards 'Guests'?

Turkey was being invaded just 150 miles away in the Dardanelles, and Turkish soldiers were being killed protecting their homeland, but no retaliation or major restrictions at all seem to have followed. She is threatened with eviction by her (Austrian, I think) landlord, and is protected from this by Turkish law! She manages to get 'British Relief' and other sums of money through the Ottoman Bank which was still trading despite being a Franco/British organisation. Her deprivations do not seem to be much greater than that of most of the locals living at her level of income.

The fact that she could take in German and/or Austrian lodgers despite earlier indications that this would not be permitted, suggests either incompetence by the city officials, or more likely that they recognised that their European allies would rather lodge with fellow-Europeans, and probably ignored or repealed earlier instructions forbidding these situations.

Marie and her mother would have lived in the European part of the city in 'Pera' – the Cihangir area I believe, and as such would not have had much contact with Turks. She does not speak of any animosity towards them. If any did exist, I suggest that she would have commented on it and might even have thought it to be reasonable under the circumstances.

There is continual reference to her 'servant', and the employment of such a person might seem an extravagance to us nowadays, but Marie would have had no cooking skills, and although she paid this woman a pittance, what would the latter have done if she had not been employed and fed? Due to the Islamic attitude to handling pork, it was natural for Christian families to have Christian servants. Such arrangements continued well into the 1950s; our 'daily' in the late 1940s when I lived in Istanbul, was a Greek Orthodox woman, and I only learned to speak Turkish by attending the English High School for Boys in the city, where the European minority were taught the language.

My grandmother would not have spoken much Turkish if any – rather like many older women from the Asian sectors, living in present-day Britain, do not speak any (or much) English. She would have spoken French or Italian to her mother, and Greek to the maid. I do not know how she learned German, but she seems to have had a good working knowledge of it. However, I feel that her native tongue was the language she thought in, as the diaries are all in excellent English. Her religion, as a Roman Catholic, is a great comfort to her. She and all the other Christians seemed to be able to attend services as and when they pleased, but of course many resident Germans and Austrians would have been Catholics as well.

She worries deeply as to the whereabouts and safety of her children, naturally enough, not knowing that at one time her sons were just some 150 miles away in the Dardanelles, and later that her husband was with them in Salonika.

Her joy at eventually seeing her sons – see pp. 68-69, must have been heart-rending.

My father managed to work through her diaries before he died in 1980 and has made certain brief notes and comments, but these are not enough to enable me fully to understand who many of the people referred to were, or how they fitted into my grandmother's circle.

My father's diaries were typed-up much later from memory, and hence there are few dates given – however, see the 'musings' on pp. 149-152.

THE IMPERIAL OTTOMAN BANK

The Ottoman Bank was founded in 1856 on the orders of Queen Victoria. For its first few years it had only a few branches, in London, Constantinople-Galata, Izmir and Beirut; but soon other branches were established in major commercial centres such as Salonika (1862), Alexandria (1866) and Paris (1868). Branches opened and closed up to the start of WWI, by which time there were over 80 of them, with some established in somewhat surprising places such as Manchester (1911), presumably to help finance the importation and payment of cotton for the many mills there and in the surrounding Lancashire mill towns.

However, with purely British funding, it could not carry out the full functions expected of an international bank, so the French were made partners in 1863, and it became truly international with its title enhanced to the more impressive 'Imperial' Ottoman Bank. This enabled it to expand to those parts of the Ottoman Empire where French was *'la langue diplomatique'*; specifically in the 'Levant' areas around Beirut and Alexandretta (now Mersin).

The Ottoman Empire was spread too far west and south for it to be able to properly administer its far-flung lands effectively, and hence various revolts were continually arising. One of these was started by Mehmet (or Mohammed) Ali, who was eventually given responsibility for Egypt, since the Sublime Porte (as the sultan's palace and responsibility was generally known – rather like 10 Downing Street), could do little about it, and bowed to the inevitable. Other subject states seeing the result of rebellions, thought to follow suit with their own rebellions.

These skirmishes and wars naturally proved expensive to run and though the Ottomans tried to raise additional funds by means of import and export taxes, these did not prove sufficient. The Crimean War (October 1853 to February 1856) proved to be the breaking point and it was realised that any further funding had to be through Western sources, partly due to the Islamic anathema towards paying any interest on loans. It was however, quite acceptable for a bank with a number of foreign directors to raise the funds.

The Ottoman Empire had not been at all involved in the industrial revolutions which had gradually spread eastwards from Western Europe, and found itself without any major manufacturing capability – its exports were mainly agricultural. However, internal demand for those goods arose but there was no capital available for their importation. Earlier there had been the *Tanzimat*' reforms of 1839 which recognised the need for re-organisation of the Empire along more Western-type lines, but these measures had not proved to be sufficient, although they did lay down the paths along which future reforms could follow.

A major turning point came in 1875 with an agreement signed between the State and the Bank which gave the latter the official ability to reform and control state finances. It also gave it exclusive rights to issue currency and appointed it official Treasurer to the Empire.

The Bank, with others, were thus able to invest in and help various major construction and engineering works and also to participate in the creation of a separate State Tobacco Monopoly. These investments in railways, banking and general commerce could be seen more to strengthen the dependence of the Ottoman economy on the capitalist European countries rather than helping local exports, though of course they did help to facilitate this trade.

During WWI the Bank was in the strange situation whereby most of its shareholders (i.e. the French and British) were at war with the Ottoman Empire and though most of the branches needed to keep open, the directors all resigned, and the ability to issue currency for the Empire was withdrawn.

During this time, and following the Armistice in 1918, some branches closed and new ones opened, reflecting the reality that the Ottoman Empire had lost most of its northern African and some of its Asian satellite states. However, the Bank managed to retain the name 'Ottoman' even though it had in 1924, to shorten its full name to simply 'The Ottoman Bank' as there was now was no longer an 'Empire'.

Following the nationalisation of the Suez Canal in 1956 it lost its Egyptian branches, but opened up some new ones in East African countries; it also started to trade in certain small Arab states and thus had a foothold when the United Arab Emirates were established in 1971, but the trend for foreign-owned businesses to revert to national ownership could not be halted and following various re-positioning of branches in other banks, in 2001 it was fully merged with the Turkish Garanti Bank.

TURKEY ENTERS THE WAR

The most-quoted reason for the Ottoman Empire to throw in its lot with the 'Central Powers' of Germany and Austro-Hungary is the fact that Winston Churchill, then a cabinet minister with the rank of First Lord of the Admiralty, decided in August 1914 not to allow the delivery of two major warships, (the new dreadnaughts) which were being built in Northern British shipyards for the Turkish Navy. The way that events were unfolding in Europe made this a very sensible decision from the Allied point of view, but it was, naturally enough, not seen that way in Turkey where the lack of a proper fighting naval fleet had led to a national appeal for funds for these ships. Public appeals for money for these ships had been made, so it could be said that the totally illegal confiscation of these ships struck home throughout the Empire. What is more, they had been largely paid for.

The Turks had seen the Dardanelles blocked by a single Greek dreadnaught, the *Averoff* during one of the recent Balkan Wars, and realised that it needed a force much greater than its small armed ships which patrolled the Aegean and Black Sea. A Turkish crew was already in the UK to take possession of the first ship – the *Resadiye*, but British soldiers were sent on board to stop this Turkish crew from boarding. The ships were incorporated into the Royal Navy after being re-named HMS *Erin* and HMS *Agincourt*.

At this point in the Introduction, it should be added that a grouping of young Turkish intellectuals seeking reforms began to establish itself in the last few years of the nineteenth century and this group, usually known in the West as the 'Young Turks', formally created a committee in 1906. They could see that the power of the Sultanate was waning and wished to ensure that their progressive views were recorded by this committee with the aim of having them imposed at some later date when the time proved right. The Young Turks had previously taken the bold step in 1902 of holding a congress in Paris and based itself in Salonika where it felt safer than being actually in Turkey. To achieve any results at all, they realised that they had to enlist some support within the army, and managed to befriend some of the officers billeted locally.

They also realised that they would have to get outside patronage from one of the Western powers and twice approached the British government to see if such support might come from this quarter. Both these overtures were rebuffed, mostly because the British ambassadors at the time were being influenced by a dragoman (Gerald Fitzmaurice) who had too much influence and a strong dislike of the Young Turks whom he saw as an unholy alliance of Freemasons and Jews – Fitzmaurice was a Catholic having earlier studied for the priesthood in Ireland.

It could be said that this illegal confiscation by Britain over the capital ships, and the rebuff from the British Government over possible support for the Young Turks' manifesto pushed Turkey into the arms of the Central Powers, but I suggest that there were certain other factors which ensured that tide would run against the Allies.

The Germans already had two powerful warships in the Mediterranean, the *Goeben* and the *Breslau*, and the British fleet in that area were given orders to intercept them, however, they failed to do so, and these both managed to get into the protected national waters of the Sea of Marmara through the Dardanelles and thence on to Constantinople. Once there, they were taken over, and the German crew given Ottoman naval uniforms. The command remained with the German officers, but the ships were renamed *Yavuz* and *Midilli*. The latter was sunk by the British in 1918 when she ventured too far out into the Aegean, but the *Yavuz* remained the flagship of the Turkish navy for some time, and I recall seeing her firing welcome salutes to British and American visiting naval fleets arriving at Istanbul in the late 1940s and early 1950s. She was however – as were all the ships from that era – a coal burner and the smoke from the funnels could be seen a long way off, and was very largely obsolete as a proper fighting ship.

My father comments on p.89 of his diaries that he had been party to a British proposal to send 10 million Turkish pounds as a loan to keep Turkey with the Allies, but Germany countered with two million pounds in gold and the ships; this offer prevailed although he claims that only one million pounds were actually received. This opinion appears to be backed-up by official records, although the amounts involved and the actual methods of payment used, differ.

Although the Imperial Ottoman Bank was Anglo/French, there were other European banks in the Empire. The Deutsche Bank had been established there in the 1890s and was largely responsible for the funding of the Constantinople (Haydar Pasha) to Baghdad railway line which was German-built. This gave German engineers and diplomats access to all the towns and cities along the route, creating good relations with local worthies. It is also suggested that the bank's interest rates were considerably lower than those of the IOB. The railway was also planned to go on to Mecca which would also give Germany *kudos* throughout the Islamic world.

In the early 1880s, German arms companies received large orders from the then Sultan Murat V, for them to supply arms following a request for Germany to advise on the modernisation of the army, and in January 1914 Field Marshal von Sanders was made Inspector-General of the Turkish army.

The Ottoman Empire's great mass across Central and Eastern Europe was a natural bastion to keep the Russian hordes separated from the Western European nations. Churchill understood this when ordering the storming of the Dardanelles with a view to taking Constantinople, as he felt that it would be relatively simple to take the capital, and then be able to advance north-west into what he called 'the naked under-belly of Austria', after possibly persuading the Russians to advance to the south-west from their borders, with the Italians advancing north-east. Of course the plan failed as the Turks fought bravely, rapidly advancing to protect the Dardanelles from the heights and sending the large Allied force packing by the end of 1915. This was considered Churchill's worse set-back and he lost his post on the War Committee.

Methods used by Turkish irregulars called *bashi-bouzouks* (translated as 'broken-heads') to put down rebellions in the 1870s in the western-most Ottoman states such as Bosnia-Herzogovina and Bulgaria, met with much criticism from British governments and created a reluctance to ally themselves too closely with the Sublime Porte. (These irregulars were not paid, but were armed by the Turks and were normally allowed to take booty).

Some of this feeling carried forward in Britain into the early twentieth century. Russia was of course always ready and able to provoke dissention, claiming to be the true protector of Christians in those Eastern European areas where Christianity was still the dominant religion despite the Islamic faith of the Ottoman rulers.

One of these Young Turks was Enver Pasha who was made War Minister in 1914; he had previously served in Berlin as Military Attaché for two years up to 1911, and thus may have developed a a pro-German bias. He soon ousted over 1000 senior and middle-ranking officers – were the ones remaining those who thought along his lines? Following the assassination of Archduke Franz Ferdinand in Sarajevo on 28 June 1914, a whole series of declarations of war ensued.

Enver had felt that Turkey was isolated and approached the German ambassador with a proposal for an alliance; although this was initially rejected, Kaiser Willhelm II – 'Kaiser Bill' over-ruled his ambassador, and a limited alliance was signed. This obliged Turkey to go to war with Russia (only) should that nation attack the Central Powers. However, there was still no complete agreement as to a full declaration of war as Enver, with his Interior Minister, Talaat Bey were waiting to see how the rapidly-moving events would evolve. But once the Germans had defeated the Russians in late August at Tannenberg in East Prussia, the die was cast and they decided to ask Germany for the money referred to on p. 89, to pay the army.

The two 'new' ships of the Turkish navy were then ordered by Enver to sail into the Black Sea in October, still under the command of German officers, and began to bombard Russian bases in the Crimea.

Once the news reached Britain, Churchill ordered the Royal Navy to attack Turkish forts on the Dardanelles peninsula, and war was declared on the Ottoman Empire on 5 November.

GREECE INVADES ASIA MINOR

The Greeks, as the natural successors to the Byzantine Empire, mainly through their religion of Christian Orthodoxism, had always considered 'Constantinople' rightfully theirs, as if the 450 years of realism that it belonged to the Ottomans through the power of conquest, did not count.

They had moved their 'Pope' – the Archbishop of the Greek Orthodox Church, back to Constantinople during the sixteenth century and had profited from the Islamic tolerance of other religions. Even today the current holder of this high office is based in Istanbul and has to be a Turkish citizen, though of course of Greek origin.

The cause of the new Hellenistic ambition in the nineteenth century could be said to be mostly due to the ambitions of one man, Eleftherios Venizelos who was born in Crete in 1864. He had as his monarch King Constantine, who had become king in 1913, and who had attended the Berlin Military Academy, obtaining an admiration of German military efficiency; also, the king had married the sister of the German Kaiser Willheim II, as most the European monarchies were similarly locked together in sometimes uneasy alliances through these marriages.

The idea of a 'Greater Greece' was always present; folksongs and ballads spoke longingly of this dream, (the *Megali* idea) rather like some folksongs in Ireland or the 'rebel' confederate states in America, and although only semi-serious, they kept the idea alive. Education also helped, with Greek schools beginning to spring up along the Asia Minor coast by the beginning of the eighteenth century, giving students a sense of pride in their culture and of kinship with their ancients.

A breed of 'Karamanli' Christians evolved who were Turkish-speaking Christian Greeks, distinguishable from the local Turks only by their religion, and through that, by their basic allegiance to Greece – a country they had never, nor would ever see.

The Greeks of Crete – then still under Ottoman rule – during one of the regular periods of national pride, rebelled in 1897 and sued for *'enosis'* (union with Greece) – a word we became familiar with in the 1950s when most of the Greek Cypriots then also declared their wish to link to the mother-country. The feeling in Athens was that this rebellion in Crete would divert Turkish troops away from the mainland, thus opening the possibility of a Greek attack overland into Thrace and Macedonia, so war was declared. The Commander for this action was the young Prince Constantine.

However, the Turks – who had recently been re-organised and re-armed by a German military mission, swiftly put down this rebellion swiftly, and Constantine was revealed as not to be up to his role as leader of the Greek forces, while the army realised that it was not capable of matching the Turks in open warfare. An International Commission was set up to adjudicate on the amount of indemnity Greece had to pay Turkey, but it did not return Thrace to the Ottomans. However, the competence of the Crown Prince had been put to the test and found wanting.

The result, though somewhat humiliating, may have left in the Greek psyche the idea that force brought some reward even if a battle was lost. The lesson was that allies were needed for future successes.

In Britain, Lloyd George was quoted as saying that the Ottoman Empire should not have any hold in Europe, suggesting that the Dardanelles should be an internationalised waterway, and even that all of Thrace (Turkey in Europe) to include Constantinople should be internationalised. (In fact both the Dardanelles and the Bosphorus are international waterways nowadays as otherwise any current Turkish government could close these passageways to the Mediterranean, Suez Canal/Red Sea and the Atlantic Ocean via Gibraltar to any nation with whom it had a quarrel – think of the USSR/Russia and the Ukraine, with their many Black Sea ports).

With the fall and control of central Asia Minor to the Seljuk Turks culminating in the capture of Byzantium/Constantinople in 1453 and the 'conversion' of many of the peasants therein to Islam over the ensuing centuries, the remaining Greek/Christian elements were concentrated in the coastal area with its access to the Aegean; this suited both parties, as the Greeks were more suited to commercial undertakings and had greater nautical ability. The new conquerors knew little of these matters and were happier as farmers, so the *status quo* remained for several centuries.

I personally recall talking to a Turkish farmer in a coastal village near Marmaris in the 1990s. "We are the farmers", he said and "they (the Greeks – pointing to an island on the horizon) are the fishermen, but we are all the same people from the Aegean. We speak some Greek, they some Turkish – we are invited over to their feast-days and they come over to ours – nobody bothers with passports. The problem now is that our children speak to the others in English".

The Anatolian peninsular remained relatively peaceful for several centuries and the Eastern Christian capital (Constantinople) thus grew in stature and magnificence over this time, whereas the Western Capital – Rome – was subject to various defeats; likewise Athens with the Slav incursions, so Constantinople gradually evolved to be the *de-facto* capital of the Hellenistic world.

With the defeat of the Ottoman Empire in 1918, various conferences were held to settle the division of the spoils. Greece as party to the victors expected its share and aimed high. Venizelos had visited London in 1918 and had produced figures showing that if the offshore Aegean islands were included (but without Cyprus and Crete), the Greeks in the coastal strip centred on Izmir/Smyrna outnumbered the Turks. He conceded that Izmir, although largely Christian, would have to become a Freeport inside the proposed Greek enclave to allow the export of wheat and dried fruit by the Turks of inner Anatolia. There was also a problem of some Greeks on the Black Sea coast – this area was too far away from Greece – or the proposed new area of 'Greater Greece' to be protected, so he suggested that this area be ceded to the new Christian state of Armenia.

Turkey – as a defeated enemy – did not take part in the Paris Conference of 1918. Britain and France appeared to support Venizelos, but the Americans did not agree, and the Italian attitude seemed to be 'what about us?'

The result for Turkey was that in May 1919, with Allied support and the protection of Allied warships, a Greek force was sent to occupy Izmir/Smyrna; the local Turkish troops were confined to barracks but as the Greeks marched through the city, a shot was fired. The Greeks returned fire and the Turks inside the barracks surrendered, but where badly treated by the invaders with some 300 to 400 casualties as the citizens from the various communities fought in the streets as law and order broke down.

The Greeks fanned out into the hinterland, and there were grisly scenes as they advanced. The inland town of Aydin was taken and left as a smoking ruin. Both sides were guilty of excesses, but the Turks were defending their homeland against a foreign power sent to subdue them.

The Turks had realised that being on the losing side in the Great War, they would have to lose some territory as indeed would the Germans, but they had not foreseen this invasion, apparently ratified by a conference where they had no representation, and they began to make plans to retaliate. By this time, their eventual leader – Mustafa Kemal (later Kemal Ataturk – father of the Turks, taking this name when he later decreed that all males should adopt a new surname), was making his mark. This man had also been a hero in the defence of the Dardanelles in 1915.

He had been appointed to a senior post in eastern Turkey which kept him out of the way of the current upheavals, and this had enabled him to bring his considerable reputation and organising ability to engineer the formation of a new government away from Constantinople and the foreigners there who had allowed this invasion of Izmir. In June he signed a protocol objecting to the Allied plans and the Sultan's meek acceptance of them.

A further treaty approved by the Sultan Mehmed VI (Sevres in 1920), awarded further Turkish territory to Greece including Adrinople/Edirne, but this treaty was not recognised by the new government now in Ankara. The Greeks realised that they had to strike at these nationalist forces or 'Kemalists' as they were sometimes known, but realised that if they advanced too far into Central Anatolia, their opponents would simply move further east to where any pursuit would stretch the Greek lines too far.

An election in Greece gave the Royalists victory which surprised everyone (my father comments on vote-rigging in p.140 in his diaries), and King Constantine became the new Head of State, to much delight in Athens. (King Alexander I had died suddenly having been bitten by a pet monkey, the wound turned septic and he succumbed within three weeks). Venizelos resigned as Prime Minister, having lost his seat, and went to Paris.

In early 1921 the Greek offensive starts seriously; troops from Bursa moving south-west and those in the south moving north-west; for the first time the Greeks encountered serious resistance for the Turks had used the winter months to reinforce certain strongholds and to train their troops. The Greeks were pushed back which gave them their first serious reversals.

In August Mustapha Kemal was made Commander-in-Chief of the Turkish Army based in Ankara and made the River Sakarya, some 40 miles south-east of the new capital, his line of defence. He was criticised for not defending the towns on the way to this line, for some were captured with great loss of life, but maintained this was the best tactic. He was totally justified, for after a three-week battle the Greeks were defeated as their supply-chain had been broken by continual harassment by Turkish forces, and they made a calamitous frontal attack on prepared positions.

The winter that followed was marked by a series of withdrawals of Greek forces from various towns which had been occupied, and by much international negotiation to try to find acceptable ways forward. The end for the Greek Army came with the battle of Dumlupinar (Tulu Pinar) in August 1922. A rapid retreat by the Greeks towards the Aegean resulted in the attack on Izmir in September. This attack, and the ensuing slaughter, whilst Allied ships in the harbour did little or nothing but watch the fires burn has been well-documented, particularly in Giles Milton's recent book 'Paradise Lost' (Sceptre 2008).

The Lausanne Conference of 1923 ensued. It first met in late 1922 and put forward a radical proposal for an exchange of populations as the only way to settle the problem of Moslems in Europe and Christians in Asia. In a way some of this had already happened with many ships calling into Aegean ports to take away desperate Greeks – mostly women and children – and return them to a homeland of which they knew little. Approximately 1.5 million Greeks migrated from Anatolia (Western Turkey) to Greece and about 500,000 Turks moved the other way.

The official communiqué confirmed the need for compulsory

exchanges, though in the case of the Greeks, many had already made the journey.

With this decree, the dream of a 'Greater Greece' was buried: the new Turkish republic was formed on 29th October, 1923, with Mustapha Kemal as its first President.

CHRONOLOGY

1900	Sept.	The Turkish Sultan (Abdul Hamid) opens a public fund to help build the Hejaz railway to the Islamic Holy Places with German assistance.
1903	Aug/Sept.	A rising against Turkish rule in Macedonia is put down with considerable force amid much protest in W. Europe.
1905	March	The Greeks in Crete revolt against Turkish rule.
1908	July	The 'Young Turks' in Macedonia openly defy the rule of the sultan; troops sent to quell the revolt, desert.
	December	First meeting of an Ottoman Parliament with a large 'Young Turk' majority.
1909	January	The Grand Vizier to the sultan is forced to resign by the Nationalists.
	April	The Turkish army revolts against the Islamic Union.
1910	December	Venizelos wins the most sets in an election for the National Assembly in Greece.
1912	April	Turkey closes the Dardanelles to international shipping; it opens again on 1 May.
	Sept.-Dec.	Balkan war between Bulgarian, Serbian, Greek and Montenegrian forces against Turkish rule – peace conference 20th December.
1913	January	Turkish garrison on island of Chios surrenders. Greeks take over. Peace conference suspended.
	February	Bulgarians renew war against Turkey.
	April/May	Turkey signs new treaty with Bulgaria.
	June	Bulgaria attacks Greece and Serbia.

	July	Turkey re-enters war; captures Adrinople from Bulgarians.
	Sept.	New treaty settles border with Bulgaria.
	November	German general von Sanders is appointed High Commander of Turkish army.
		Greek-Turkish peace treaty with several Aegean islands including Crete passing to Greek control.
1914	June	Greece annexes three further Aegean islands.
	August	1st – German-Turkish treaty signed.
		4th – Britain declares war on Germany
		12th – on Austria/Hungary.
		Two capital German ships (*Goeben* and *Breslau*) manage to evade British ships in Eastern Mediterranean, and enter Turkish waters where they replace new ships held back by Britain.
	October	1st – Turkey closes the Dardanelles.
		29th – Turkish warships under German command bombard Russian Black Sea ports.
	November	2nd – Russia declares war on Turkey.
		5th – France and Britain declare war on Turkey.
1915	March	British and French ships unsuccessfully attempt to storm the Dardanelles; three ships sunk.
	April	Allied landings on the Gallipoli peninsula with the intention of advancing to and capturing Constantinople.
	May	Turkish government decides to deport some 1.8 million Armenians from Eastern Turkey fearing that they (as Christians) will side with the Russians allowing an attack from the East.
	August	Italy declares war on Turkey.
	Sept.	Bulgaria signs military agreement with Germany and Turkey.
		Greek army is mobilised.

1916	January	Final allied forces withdrawal from Gallipoli peninsula.
	March	Allies agree to partition Turkey.
	August	Turkey declares war on Russia.
1917	January	Turkey denounces earlier treaties which had defined their 'new' boundaries.
	February	USA breaks off diplomatic relations with Germany.
	April	USA and Turkey sever relations.
	June	US Troops land in France.
1918	July	Execution of the Russian Royal Family (Ex Tsar Nicholas II and family).
	Sept.	Collapse of Turkish resistance in Palestine.
	October	14th – Turks pass a message to US. President Wilson proposing an armistice.
		30th – Allies sign armistice with Turkey.
	November	1st – British and French forces enter Constantinople.
		11th – Armistice between Allies and Germany in place.
1919	February	President Wilson puts forward the League of Nations proposal to the Paris Peace Conference – adopted 25th March.
	May	A Greek force supported by Allied ships occupies the major Aegean port of Smyrna/Izmir in Asia Minor.
	June	Mustafa Kemal and other Turkish nationalist leaders sign an agreement declaring resistance to the Allies' plans for Turkey, and the sultan's meek acceptance of them (The National Pact).
	July	Congress held in Erzurum in Eastern Turkey under the leadership of Mustapha Kemal to resist Allied plans for the dismemberment of the Ottoman Empire.
1920	February	Allies announce that Turkey will retain Istanbul, but that the Dardanelles will come under international control.

	March	The sultan closes the Istanbul parliament; some nationalists are arrested, other escape to join their Ankara colleagues.
	April	Opening of a new Turkish assembly with Mustapha Kemal as the new president.
	May	Former Ottoman Empire territories are assigned to Britain and France.
	July	The Greeks under their new King Alexander occupy Adrinople/Edirne.
	August	Treaty of Sevres awards parts of Turkey to the Greeks.
1921	January	Greeks attack in Anatolia starting a Greek-Turkish war.
	February	A London conference between the Allies, the Turkish Nationalists and representatives of the sultan's government.
	April	Following Turkish victories in Anatolia, the Greeks withdraw.
	July	Greeks invade again pressing North-East towards Ankara.
	August	Greeks defeated at Battle of Sakarya, and retreat back to the coast.
	October	13th – Russia recognises the new Ankara government. 20th – France also signs agreement with Ankara.
1922	March	Allied conference in Paris recommends that Greece and Turkey should sign an armistice.
	July	The Greek leaders in Smyrna/Izmir declare autonomy for the Greek-speaking parts of Anatolia.
	August	Turks defeat the Greeks at the Battle of Afyon.
	Sept.	Turks take Izmir from the Greeks – many Greeks killed.
	October	1st – A new Turkish constitution abolishes the sultanate.

	October	13th – An armistice ends the Greek-Turkish war.
	November	1st – Kemal Pasha proclaims a Turkish republic
		17th – The former sultan leaves Turkey.
1923	July	Following the Treaty of Lausanne, 1.5 million Greeks migrate from Turkish territory to Greece and .5 million Turks move from land ceded to Greece, back to Turkey.
	October	Mustafa Kemal is elected president of the new republic.
1924	March	The new assembly declares Turkey to be a secular state.

Part One:
THE DIARIES OF
MRS MARIE LYSTER
(1865–1965)

Volume 1, February 1916

(Editor's note: all my own additions are in square brackets) - thus [ ].

22nd February 1916

I have made up my mind to write a few lines every day, so far I was afraid of doing so for fear of the authorities coming to search, but so far nothing of the kind having taken place I shall note down what goes with us and hope it will not get me into trouble.

Simon [the *kapici* or concierge/janitor] now often has to pay as much as 18 piastres a day for bread. Soldiers sell their bread at 6 pts the loaf and very many people have to pay this exorbitant price so as to feed their families. So far we have not paid for bread at fancy prices.

I have obtained a *vesika* [residential permit] from our police station for mother who is old and infirm. The servant heard of this in the morning, and I was hastening to find out if it was true. I happened to meet M. Lactec [?] who came with me, but I could have managed alone. I am getting a regular business woman! Poor me! I wish I had my poor hubby to do all my business for me. I wonder how this *vesika* works.

Another vital question besides the bread is getting change; yesterday all my fortune was 1½ paras [40 paras = 1 *piastre*], so I went out and borrowed 2 pts from the xxxx so as to give it to the servant to take with her. It seems however that Lt¼ notes (paper) have been issued so that it might be easier to change. I went out at about 9 to find a way of getting change. I tried four different shops but had to go to Harty[*see page 74] where things are a bit dearer. I felt quite miserable at having to pay 23½ for 4 *okes* [an *oke* was an Ottoman measure of weight – about 3 lbs,] of potatoes,

1 oke of canary seed, 4 *galetas* [a sort of hard biscuit] and 3 eggs. I would have paid about 8 pts for that in ordinary times – at those prices, we will have to be very hungry before we eat them.

On my return I looked after the canaries and worked in Mama's room till lunch time after which I went to see about the bread – it seems that bread ran out at 9 this morning, so my walk proved to be useless apart from the fact that I now know what time to send Efstaffia [the maid] out tomorrow.

Friday: I did not write yesterday. Tomorrow I will go out at seven, leaving Mama in bed. Yesterday, I went for a walk down Tophane and up past the German Embassy; it took me about 1½ hours. It was lovely weather. It being early I hardly met any women, and of course no ladies. With a companion, one like me enjoys their society, but not one's walk.

My mother and I have little to say to each other, except to wonder what our dear ones are doing. Nina [a Mme. Primi] comes to see us often; she is very hard up poor thing and has great trouble with all the economies we have to make. Mr Jalls [? a neighbour] had promised to help her, but he left last week – it seems that his trip to Italy will be very difficult and even dangerous. The Allies, even if expelled have very little means of getting away, so we are really shut in.

28th. Efstaffia [the maid] went to see her mother and was present when a soldier offered his bread ration for 8 pts. Men and women were disputing who would have it. I went to the bank to get a paper pound changed into piastres. I owed the washerwoman 30 pts. I gave the same sum to the servant; I will keep the other money to pay the porter's salary – money flies. I am wondering if the bank will continue to pay Alfred now he has been absent from his post a year. It would come very hard if this happened. I wish we could have news; it is a month since the last, and Henry's [her eldest son – my father] letter is dated 21st December.

I am getting disheartened at hearing of the German victories in France. Mr Appell [? – a German who was taking English lessons from her]; came, he was in full uniform, he has been in the army since 1914, first in Russia, then in Serbia and also at the

Dardanelles; he said that the British left many good things behind there, and that their papers (British ones) as well as the French ones speak of food riots in Germany on account of the shortages; that this is not true. No one in Germany is hungry. He was very circumspect when asked how many soldiers were with him. He has been promoted to 1st lieutenant, and has a gold Austrian medal and a Turkish ribbon. With all this news, I feel very sad – when will this wretched war end?

29th. Sylvia Macarthy [an old friend who gave English lessons], came in the morning and brought a loaf which she could spare; she also taught me how to crochet. She gave me a pattern and wrote down the stitches so that I managed it after a little fumbling. I had wanted to learn this as it is a useful and amusing way to work. [I remember her still crocheting in her 90s].

March 1st. After lunch today I went to the bank to get my Lts.15 [presumably an allowance or salary from her husband]. It seems that the directors have made an arrangement with some big grocer who is to supply their clerks with goods at wholesale prices. However cheaply things are sold, they are still frightfully dear. I do not understand why I do not get news. I keep telling them that they could write to Virginie [?] and I could get their news this way [?]. Henry might also write pc's from Salonika as other boys do.

March 5th. Yesterday I went down to the bank to see about provisions. I waited for nearly 2 hours. A Turkish lady came in also to have a letter written, and she smoked all the time leaving her cigarette ends to burn out in the ash-tray. I could stand it no more and left, and on the way out met Mr. Castopoulos [?] who was very nice and arranged things for me. He said that if he had known the trouble he would have with this business, he would never have started it. It seems he gets more complaints than thanks. Tomorrow will be dear Henry's birthday. Where is he? What is he doing? – this war seems endless. It seems that Sweden has now turned against us, and here it is hoped that Roumania will follow suit. Another ship has gone down with troops; this is worse than dying on the battlefield. God spare my poor Henry; if I knew his address and regiment I might write to him. He is 28 now and Freddy will be 19 – both have been good boys and I pray that God will keep them honest and pious men who will marry Christian wives who will be helpmates to them and good mothers for their children. I think they both love and respect me which is a very pleasant feeling.

12th March. There are [sic] no news to buoy us up – on the contrary, it seems that a fort near Verdun has fallen. Some people persist in being pessimistic. Our butcher, amongst others, says that we will have peace by May. When I repeat this to Mama, she laughs. They know no less than others do; nobody has any news and we all repeat what rumours get about. Few of us rely on what the papers say, even the foreign ones do not give the truth.

March 18th. A few days ago a whole lot of people were arrested as they managed to get their letters to Italy through some clerks of the Greek Embassy who travelled with the Greek diplomatic service bag. They are all in prison pending their trial and should it be proved that they talked politics in their correspondence, it will go badly with them. I pity their families, but why do they want to talk of things which they know nothing about?

March 26th. I was summoned to the A.C. [? Austrian Consulate] to receive a communication. I dressed in my best as one has to impress the small fry in the office or they look down on one and make one wait. I was very disappointed as it was a sort of circular letter from Alexandria [?] wanting news of myself and mother. I told them to reply that we were well.

April 2nd. I have not written for a week, but do so little that I find it needless to write. One day is exactly like another.

30th April. I had letters of the 21st which had left my dear ones on the 10th, so were of recent date. The life Henry [her eldest son, my father] is leading is just the one I would wish for him, except for the risk which is great and constant. [He was working with the Greek Irregulars in Intelligence – see his own diaries, pp. 101-122.]

He will not become rich this way, but being in the bank [Ottoman Bank, like his father,] would not make him rich either. He is not made for business.

May 17th. There is no doubt that Mama has not the strength she had a year ago on the 15th May when she had her accident. [This is the only reference to my belief that the old lady had had a fall which prevented her travelling away from Turkey; but this would still have been in 1915, some nine months after the declarations of war in August 1914].

20th. [My grandmother dismisses her servant Efstaffia; reasons too complicated to explain].

June 2nd. Yesterday was the 29th anniversary of our wedding. I feel certain dear Alfred thought of me. Whatever happens in this dreadful war, we will not see another one. There are great tales of peace – God speed them. What a blank is the future. Will Alfred return to his post – will Henry be spared, and will Freddy [her younger son, my uncle] abandon his new career – What will Tizza [her daughter Edythe] do? God will ordain for the best. I feel confident for He has visibly helped us in all our difficulties.

June 5th. I am expecting a new servant; I have been some days without and the house feels it in the way of sweeping and cleaning, but my pocket feels it as well.

June 10th. What trouble for dear England! A naval battle at Skaggerak with the loss of so many ships and men. And yesterday the loss of the *Hampshire* with Lord Kitchener on board with all his staff. It is very depressing – God give rest to all those poor sailors. I dread lest Arthur's boys should be amongst the numbers. [This must be a reference to her brother-in-law, Arthur Edward Lyster, then of Great Baddow, Essex, who had three sons and a daughter. The eldest was then Lt. RN. Arthur Lumley St. George Lyster who did survive the war and during WWII rose to the rank of Rear Admiral, Aircraft Carriers. The fact that she refers to him as 'Arthur', suggests that she did know him, or of his then position.]

With the announcement of the naval battle, all the flags were hoisted and their victory proclaimed in the papers and at the German club – I felt wretched. What an end to such an eventful life. There was a rumour that he [Lord Kitchener] had been saved, but I fear unkindly that it was not true. I am under the impression that it was on the *Hampshire* that Tizza dined with some officers and some other girls. How she enjoyed her evening, and how happy I was to let her go. All in England must feel the loss.

June 12th. I have taken on an old woman [Catrina] who was in great want and looking for a situation to keep herself alive. She is honest, clean, looks decent and is only paid 60 pts.

There was a fire near Taksim [a central square in the European quarter], and not being insured I got nervous for the next occasion and I have sent word to the firm to send someone to insure us for Lts. 900, but only for 6 months otherwise I shall be hard up.

June 21st. What heat! It has been stifling here. We have been told that all foreigners had to appear with their papers and two photos to be registered. I had not taken my American passport as it had been previously registered and I thought that it would not be required, so being asked for it, I had to come home and go out again On seeing Mrs A.J. Lyster he declared that the passport was not mine because I told him that my name was Marie; with difficulty I got him to understand that it was mine.

July 5th. The heat is still terrific – those poor fellows fighting. I wonder if my dear ones get cards. Very likely their papers are full of our having cholera here. I hope it does not make them anxious for it is not so – it is the normal summer *cholerine* [?]. We have been told that unless we are vaccinated, we would not have our bread permits renewed. I am trying to get Mama exemption as I do not think she is fit enough to be experimented on. I decided to ask a Greek military doctor who called on the others in the apartment block, to get exemption for Mama and advice for me, as the man issuing the bread permits was still making difficulties. He said that Mama was certainly exempt, had a wonderful heart for her age, but mine was not very satisfactory. I had the serum which operation did not hurt at all, but there was no mention of vaccination papers – those who have them have not been asked for them, and we now get our bread regularly.

July 20th. I was going to spend my last pound on quite a lot of things I required, and was wondering what I could do to tide over the ten days till the end of the month. In had made my mind to sell some stationery which was left in the desk we had bought. I had written to Alfred asking for a little more to make up for the pound that I had spent on the insurance – who knows if he will get it either through Lausanne or Bucharest, and if so when he will act, then I noticed some playing cards in Alfred's drawer and of which I had heard there was a dearth, and behind them was a small sealed box which I did not hesitate to open. What a blessing and what a relief! It contained two Turkish and one English pound. I felt inclined to kiss them like a long-lost friend. I know that Alfred had put them aside as specimens of gold struck during the sultan's visit to Brousa [Brusa] and Adrinople [Edirne]; the English pound was of 1824. God is very good to me, I am never grateful enough. I gave a silver 9pts piece which I also found in the box to St. Anthony [patron saint of lost items!]. What a pleasure and luxury to be able to give! I must now see what I can get for my gold for it is at a premium. I shall keep the English gold for I hope that I will not need it this month.

July 28th. I went to the American Embassy and sent a message to Alfred saying that we were well; also one to Henry; it will have to go through Berne. I mentioned in Alfred's message that Mother was ageing. In my correspondence I cannot say this as it might be taken to apply to our country.

Charcoal has gone up; Harty [*] will not accept new orders, but promised to see what he could do for us. I have only one tin of petroleum [?kerosene/paraffin] from the old stock, I dare not think of the winter with no fuel for heating. Many people have bought wood at 115 the *cheki* [an Arabic/Ottoman measure of weight/cubic capacity, approximating to a cart-full]. There may be one *cheki* left in the cellar; I put off going to see for fear there may be less. We burnt very little last year, so there may be more. Sunday

will be the anniversary of the declaration of war. Our good father
the Pope has ordered that all children the world through should
take holy communion. I think this is a splendid idea, as God in his
goodness will surely listen to those little ones, so may of whom
have fathers at the war.

August 2nd. The latest scare is that the belligerents [presumably
meaning local Axis families] of Candilli [a village on the Asiatic
side of the Bosphorus], have been given 48 hours to leave. One old
lady there has not left her house for fifty years. It will come hard
on them to leave; all they have is their small house and the few
things it contains. The Prinkipo [the largest of the 4 inhabited
islands in the Sea of Marmara, close to the city – now called
Buyukada] people have also had notice to leave, but somehow or
other a good few are still there; only those who believed in the
order hurried away, the rest lingered and hope to stay on.

August 6th. Dear Tizza's birthday! God bless her. It was a Sunday
when she was born just as the angelus was ringing at midday. [The
angelus is a Roman Catholic call to prayer by means of a bell rung
three times a day; 6 in the morning; at mid-day and at 6 pm.] She
was smaller than Henry and particularily poor Leslie [a son who
was stillborn], so that I was disappointed, but I was told it was so
with girls. Dear Dr. Patterson was so kind; Alfred had hoped for
a girl and so we telegraphed 'Edith and Marie send love' [not
'Edythe' here.] Our cradle being at Phillippopolis, and the
bassinette which we had left here and on which we counted for
the baby having disappeared, we had to put a little mattress into a
drawer which we rested on two chairs. It made a very comfortable
cot and the baby was happy. [The 'Lyster' family book privately
published in 1913 by the Revd. H.L. Lyster Denny, gives the
information on p. 61, "James Leslie, b.1891, died as an infant in
Phillippopolis, Bulgaria". I cannot trace a place with this name in
either of my atlases, nor can explain why my grandmother was
there, presumably without her husband].

August 10th. The danger of having no bread is looming again.
Should Roumania close the frontier we shall go hungry again.

What a winter lies before us if things do not settle. Some people say it cannot last over the next few months, that some of the fighters will have to give in, others that being a question of life or death for our opponents, they will hold out to the bitter end. Meanwhile so many young fellows are falling. To occupy my mind I am arranging Alfred's stamps which I found in pockets, boxes and drawers. I shall then arrange Freddie's.

August 12th. Was called to the US Embassy. Whilst waiting had a talk with Jim Fatherall [?] who had just been let out of prison; there were eight of them and four are still there, so he had come to intercede for them. He said that if four of them had to be locked up, all the British should take it in turn – there are about 450 of them. I was not allowed to take away my letters but had to read them there. I hurriedly read Alfred's [her husband] and Freddie's few lines and smuggled Tizza's into my bag! I know it was an abuse of confidence, but I wanted to read it to Mama, and this rule is made for form's sake – they do not mind I am certain. I asked if I could return and read the letters a second time, and will return Tizza's letter to the envelope. I hope they will not notice my cheating. Freddie seemed in high spirits; he is now a 2nd lieutenant interpreter to the Intelligence Dept. I feel safer knowing him in England. Tizza says she had a letter from a friend in France saying he hoped that Freddie would not be sent where he was as it was a veritable hell. She has been promoted and likes her work and extra pay.

August 15th. Assumption – the bells are ringing for High Mass. I see that at last the Salonika forces are going to move. I expected it a long time ago. I suppose that Freddy is longing to see some fighting. I suppose that Henry's work is the most dangerous, riding about for news and orders.

27th. It seems that Jim Fatherall and Co. who were released have been arrested again and will be sent away. Poor things; it was a short-lived joy.

August 28th. Roumania has declared war on Austria and Germany and Turkey take part [sic] for their ally [?]. There was a great commotion the day the news was posted, particularly at the grocer's shops. One lady rushed in and ordered a large sack of potatoes; being from a small family, Mr Harty told her "Madam, think it over, and come back tomorrow, for the potatoes I sell will not keep and you may have to throw half away which would be a waste".

Sept. 2nd. The *vesika* bread is awful. [*vesika* being the local identity document, perhaps those with these *vesikas* were only allowed a certain type of bread]. It is canary yellow, is heavy like lead being made with maize, husks and all so that it is most indigestible. It crumbles to the slightest touch.

8th. Yesterday evening the town was beflagged; there has been a victory over the Roumanians and the taking of the town of Orsova. The Ferri's providing me with a paper. I consider it wasteful to buy one, but I suffer for this little privation for though awfully kind in every way, they do not realise how they torment me by not letting me have the news in the mornings. Yesterday I could not go out, and no one came and so I did not even know what Greece was doing. The servant told me of the flags and quite late I mustered up courage and sent for the papers, but it was a late telegram that brought the news and so even now at 10a.m. I do not know the real news.

Sept. 17th. I have received according to Alfred's promise, twenty-one pounds; *ie.* English pounds. It is very nice to feel one has a husband who though far away, still provides for one. I shall have an English lesson twice a week for 125 pts which will be very welcome, as it will be my own earning. Mrs Kalcheff [?] whose daughter is at the American school wants to learn English as a surprise for her husband; she is very small and pretty and I am sure I will enjoy the lessons.

27th. Time is passing and no solutions yet. All seem to wish for peace but no-one sues for it for the consequences would be appalling for the vanquished, so both parties go on fighting till they both are drained to the core. Some say that after Europe has laid down her arms in sheer weakness, the yellow peril, so long talked of, will approach and finish us off. Then I suppose it will be the end of the world. Thank God that we will not be alive then, not even our children I hope. [This presumably means 'the Chinese'].

October 6th. I went to the cellar, and thank God there is enough wood to last us for some time if we are very economical and we do not have a very cold winter.

October 9th. Ettore Alanta [?] came to see us yesterday; he is immense; what a contrast to our boys; he is forty and they are in their first youth, but much as he would like to remain here he is afraid of being taken for his military service so prefers to return to his little hole. He says *'on tient a sa peau après tout'* [one hangs onto one's own skin.] There is very little patriotism amongst the Austrians that I know – they all go under compulsion; unless fired by youth, no one would budge I believe. It is a mad thing to bring up one's children as the apple of one's eye and then send them to be slaughtered or maimed. It is against common sense.

19th. With electricity at our door, all our road is lighted [sic]; before the municipality obliged our landlady to light her door one felt like going into chaos when approaching our street. Many other houses have electricity which is a luxury, and does not cost very dear, but does need a good initial expense. In our flat it would cost about St. (£) 9 I believe; one must be flush to pay so much at one time. Above and below us they have taken in electricity. Now and then there is a scare that lacking coal, the company will have to stop giving light. So far it has been only rumours.

I have given up concerning dear Tizza's letters – it is an awful shame. I am certain she said nothing which the censors would disapprove of. Mama has been very irritable recently; so many subjects of conversation are so laboured that it is difficult to find something to say. She was always prejudiced and now finds fault with everyone and everything; although old and infirm she cannot make up her mind to accept things as they are.

October 29th. The Allies victory in Roumania has been a great show, but victory seems further off than ever. Writing last Xmas, Freddie wrote "the consolation is that we will not spend another winter away from home". I suppose that we will all say the same again, but let us hope with more chance of it coming true. It will be impossible I suppose for 1917 to be a full year of war. There is a persistent rumour that all belligerents are to be turned out. I don't suppose that single women would be affected, but still it would not be nice to remain alone.

Nov. 1st. I have again lost an old card case with 5 pts. I who try and save a few *paras* seem destined to spend my money by losing it!

November 5th. This morning two Austrian soldiers, our neighbours, were marched away handcuffed between two others with guns and an officer following. What could the poor wretches have done? It must be very hard for some of them are no longer young, accustomed to rule in their households and even in business, to have to obey officers who very likely are their inferiors in intelligence and birth.

Poland has been proclaimed a kingdom.

7th November. Coming home from church this morning, I saw a detachment of German soldiers at the top of our street. They looked muddy, dusty and so tired; they carried all sorts of things on their backs, bulky and heavy. I think everybody pitied them. When near our door, I saw one sit down in the road with all his impedimenta beside him. He seemed dead-beat so I took a chair out of the hall and asked him to sit down which he did. He seemed so happy to have this chair to sit on. I then ran upstairs and took him a glass of wine which he enjoyed very much. He said they had not slept all night. I did not like to ask him where they came from. He said that he had rheumatism in all his joints caught in the trenches in Gallipoli and that they were now on their way home.

He was about 50 I should say. His wife had died in May last and he had seven children. I asked him if he knew where he had to go and he said that a comrade was coming to fetch him, so I left him, but shortly afterwards Rosa [? a maid or neighbour] came saying he wanted me. I thought he just wanted to thank me, and felt it exaggerated politeness, but no, the poor man was in a fix about joining the others. He said that they had to go to a Greek school, so I presumed that it must be the [word illegible], so I put my hat on, suggested that he left his baggage under Rosa's care, and taking his stick we started off, but had hardly started when he saw one of his friends who was coming for him, so we returned and the two of them shouldered his bags, and left after thanking me profusely. I wonder if he thought I was German. [My father once told me that his mother spoke reasonable German.] He was a common man though very polite.

The Germans are going to build a Catholic Church and this will cost them about Lts.60,000. They want to spread their influence. I saw in a German paper that the Emperor, when passing through Cologne had gone into the cathedral and had been found 'in prayer'. I don't doubt his religious feelings, but what an actor he is! What a '*poseur*'.

12th. Yesterday evening quite late, I got a note from Mr Frero [?] asking for a subscription for "the civil prisoners of war who are suffering in our stead"; there were so far few names down, but those who had given from Lt.3 to Lt.½; only one person had given 90 pts, so I did likewise. Of course it is to get them something for Xmas. Then I had a note from Mr. Philip of the American Embassy asking me to go to his office the next day so as to decide about sending Xmas presents to the prisoners of war. He had evidently picked out a few ladies for we were only ten. The fund was rich with over Lt 700. It was a question of what to send. It seems that there are over 2000 men and officers with 5 generals and 7 colonels for whom we will try to make plum puddings, cakes and toffees. The money comes from well-wishers in England.

22nd Nov. For my share, I have been given 5 loaves to grate for the plum puddings, not much. I also have some 100 old stock of books and magazines which I will send to the poor soldiers, but they must be called for and censored and I hope they will be collected in time.

The Austrian Emperor [Franz Joseph] died this morning; the

papers had just mentioned that he had been unwell, but when I saw the flags at half-mast at the Embassy I guessed what it was for.

November 23rd. I thought it would be wise to lay out from Lts.4 or 5 for just two electric burners, as I am dreading having to go without lights as petroleum [paraffin/kerosene] is getting so scare, so today I was to have a visit from two electricians, but last night Mr. Ferri [?] told me that permission to instal electricity had been withdrawn, so we will have to manage as best we can. Sugar has gone up, as Austria is not sending any more as it now can be used as an explosive!

December 9th. Here we are in the last month of the year. This winter so far, we have not needed a fire. Today is lovely weather, but most of our thoughts are on the future as the news is not good. Another capital gone! [this presumably refers to the fall of Bucharest on 30 November] and Greece upside down against us. The few who are optimists give us hope, but it looks very dark around. I have had a rather big disappointment as an order has come that no foreign gold was to be paid so all our salaries would come down to just the bare amount.

December 17th. There was been a proposition of peace sent by the Central Powers, but it will most likely not be accepted. I got a message off to my dear ones from the US Consulate. I hope they will get it about New Year 1917.

21st December. My birthday – poor me! Arrests are in the air again. 12 Italians have been arrested and the other belligerents are wondering if their turn will come; general expulsion is again on the 'tapes' [?], but I do not suppose females alone will be worried.

Dec. 26th. Christmas Day has passed, very quietly and sadly. The belligerents were given permission to attend the midnight services, so the churches were full. [There was a general 10 pm curfew in operation.] We went to bed as usual, but heard the 'Gloria' bells which are very impressive in a still night. Before lunch, Sylvia [a friend] came with some holly, mistletoe and cakes. I gave the servant 40 pts and Tizza's school uniform dress. It was a bit too much, but she is a poor girl [!] and needed a dress badly.

Two of the old Italians were released and two younger ones taken in their stead. Poor Mr Frero [?] was arrested and taken away for deportation, but the Americans just managed to stop it, so he is now in prison with the other Englishmen. It seems an *iman* was arrested in Manchester.

28th. Peace is still talked of, but I do not see how it can come about; I don't see what Wilson [US President Woodrow Wilson] had to have a say for now unless he was asked to do so. Greece seems in as great a pickle as ever.

I answered an advertisement of a German lady wanting English conversational lessons, but so far have had no answer. I do not think I am acting wrong in teaching English. The English prisoners were let out for 24 hours on Xmas day. Our Austrian military neighbours had grand doings on Xmas eve. I saw any amount of cakes carried to them, then lots of meat and vegetables; also 2 barrels of beer. It was a fine night and they sang and 'noshed' till about 9.1/2. I had also seen a Xmas tree go into the house. They seemed very merry, but who knows how many had heavy hearts!

1917

Jan 2nd 1917. God bless the New Year. Let us hope it will be a happy year for everyone. I pray it will see the end of the war for it is hardly possible that it will continue another whole year. I suppose we will see interesting events which will be marked in history. It seems England refused America's offer of mediation, as well as Germany's offer of peace; that America will insist on Germany's accepting the terms upon which the Allies would accept a Peace Conference etc. All this I heard yesterday; today I have not seen a paper.

The way prices are going up is quite distressing. Nevertheless the upper tiers give fine teas, dinners and Xmas trees – the pastry cooks are full of good things and clients, and smaller shops which sell trimmings, flowers etc. are making heaps of money. Mrs Dickson [?] whose brother-in-law has a shop told a friend that she had never made as much money since the war. Why?

The other day a respectable-looking man came close to me in the street and whispered that he used to be Alfred's hairdresser; that he was so pleased to see me and asked for news of his client. I said that I would have been pleased to see him. He replied that he had thought of calling on me but was afraid as I was English. Fancy people being afraid of going into an Austrian apartment [block] and ringing on our door on the third floor.

Last evening I went down to the Scheffer's [?]. It was quite a treat. I have for so long been deprived of meeting more than a couple of people at a time. I see nothing young and pretty, never hear music.

14th. Yesterday Père Apollinaire came to see us. He had been blessing homes for the Epiphany [6th January]. They count 6,000 souls in St. Marie's parish. I had no idea there were so many Catholics in this parish. He said he went into homes that were not fit to herd cattle, and that he had no idea there could be such a lack of necessaries in a human habitation – he is Belgian.

17th. Rumours of famine are persistent; we have heard them before, but if there is not actual famine, food will be at famine prices.

January 20th. Yesterday in the paper amongst the list of guests dining at the American Embassy was the name of Henry Newbolt as military attaché. I do not for a moment think that he is a relation to our Newbolts, but in a spirit of adventure and to vary my life a bit, I shall go and see him – if my courage will take me to his door.

There is a certain feeling of terror in the atmosphere; in the market last night people really looked scared; prices go up twice a day. Wealthy people fill the grocer's shops and the poor look on in despair. I have already seen two people sitting or lying down in the street played out. People surrounded them and tried to help but I doubt if they could give them life.

January 21st. I put on my best and went to the American Embassy making up my mind that I would plunge into this Newbolt business. All my visiting cards were finished and not requiring any for calling I use 'Mr. Fred. Lyster's' for ordinary purposes, scratching out Freddie's name and writing mine, but of course that would not do for a first call at an embassy. I was lucky, for I found a [proper] card in my Easter book [?],sent it in, and was ushered into a room, and a pleasant nice man came forward holding my card asking me to be seated. He is charming, but of course no relation. I said that my mother, Mrs Henry Newbolt was an old lady and an invalid, and seeing his name fancied that he might be a relative. He was much amused by the similarity of name and I told him what I knew of Papa's family. He took down our address and said he would call on us the next day.

I thought I would titivate myself and Mama a bit for his visit and tell the servant how to behave, but hardly had we had our tea when a gentleman was announced, and though it was getting dusk he was put into the drawing room without a light. He must have made a mistake about the day. There was just light enough to show him some family photos. He is very nice and unaffected. I quite enjoyed his visit. He did not stay long and promised to come again. He is a major.

January 29th. All the recent price rises shatters one's nerves; then the wine man came and said from the 1st [February] wine would be 16 pts. It is the only extra we have; no cheese, no fruit, no sweets, no coffee. I shall grin and go on taking it; only ¾'s a wine glass after all.

I have made up my mind to let Tizza's room and have written to Mrs Hazel [?] as she knows many Austrians. I told her that if I found a lodger I would put in electricity and she is anxious that I should do so, she may look out for someone. I have told many people about lessons, but have had none so far.

Feb. 4th. I told Miss Pears about a lodger; she has two Americans and also Mr Harty. It seems that German and Austrian officials are not allowed to lodge with belligerents. Submarine war has been declared by Germany. I suppose it will bring things to a climax.

February 10th. America has broken off relations with Germany, but war has not been declared; we are all wondering how this will affect us, should the American Embassy have to leave. I have written to Major Newbolt; we felt a certain amount of safety under their protection.

12th. I have come to my last pound; where will I turn to for money? I had a signed photo of Garibaldi which I gave to Nina to sell – she says they offered 100 [?pts or pds.] I might have more in good times, but these being bad times I told her to sell it. Maybe she will bring me the money before I have none left.

15th Feb. Yesterday I went to Mrs Ledieuer [?]; she has her house full of lodgers, mostly officers so I though she might help me. One of the officer's servants came in to ask for something, so I interpreted and then asked how things were – 'splendid,' he said. "England wanted to starve us and now very shortly we will starve them – she only has food for four weeks: we have sunk so many tons [of shipping] that soon she will have no ships left, and then it will be peace" I said "who will be the victors?" "There is no doubt" he replied, "it will be a grand peace for us this time; we offered peace, it was refused and now she will be sorry". He did not speak of the other nations. He had five brothers, all serving (the wives get 36 marks a month and the children 12). They grew their own vegetables, had pigs, so for them they did not feel any want. He is from Hanover on the Westphalian frontier. The officers all expect the end of the war in about six months – "When we have reduced England".

I hear that 145 ships have been sunk in one week.

23rd. Yesterday an Austrian officer came to see the room, but as I was out, he said he would come back again, so I will have to remain indoors for a while. I believe I am to have little Saviero for English; they wanted me to give her music lessons as well, but I do not feel equal to it after all these years.

How dreadful that with nearly Lt.20 [a month?], two people and a servant, I have to practice economy to its utmost limit.

March 3rd. I have started my new lesson – I am to get Lt.1½. No lodger, and the electricity question will have to be solved. I have seen three men who ask from 6 to 12 Lts. The one that will undertake the two lights for Lt.7 will do three for Lt.9.

Mr Frero [?] has given supplies to the British colony at half price, so I have bought-in for 153 pts., which means no money for electricity. Granny had many people visiting her for her fête-day [no age mentioned].

4th March. Poor Noelie Dussi has lost her son; he was two months older than Freddie; they are Italians. She had sent him away at the first exodus when Bulgaria declared against us. He died in a sanatorium in Switzerland. Luckily she has a daughter who seems strong.

March 5th. Today America will come to a decision. Presently I will have to dress for Saviero's lesson. It is rather a nuisance, but I will rejoice when I get paid.

March 6th and 9th. The 6th was dear Henry's 29th birthday, and today is Freddie's 20th. How happy I would be to know how they are. The best time I had with him [Henry] was taking him to England. [no dates known]. I will never forget the affectionate and trusting way he held my hand when we left him at Woodford Station on our way home where he was to go to school.

March 13th. The electricity people are here and both lamps will be ready by this evening. When we get the current in is another thing. I do not know if I have acted wisely for the 6½ Lts is a fortune during these hard times. I hope to get Lt.1 for the Garibaldi photo and another Lt.1 for the 10 frs. papal piece.

March 14th. We have not eaten meat for ten days, nor have many like us. I must admit that I miss it, but who can afford 43pts for lamb, 36 for beef and 48 for mutton? Fish is also out of the question. It would be like eating gold. We have had no water for four days; we only have it one or two days a week. Luckily there is a cistern in the house, and as we have had a great deal of rain, there is a good supply in case of need – others have to buy water.

March 17th. Russia seems to be in effervesence. I wonder if it will make any difference in events. Of course little by little we will see the result. How splendid if it favourably hastened the end. [The Tsar abdicated on the 15th, and his brother Grand Duke Michael refused the throne, ending the Romanov dynasty's rule].

March 18th. I have a chance of a demand for a canary. I have asked 100 pts and do not know if I will get it, but I pity the poor little thing. I also want to sell some Bulgarian stamps, but one has to rely on one's friends and cannot hurry them up. I must make up my mind not to rely on what one hopes to sell.

March 21st. Last night our electric lamps being in order, we lighted [sic] them which was very pleasant, but what was not pleasant was that instead of having to pay 23 pts. monthly, it will be 38, plus the 50 pts. left as a deposit. I gave the canary on trial, but as I know it sings very well, I hope they will soon bring the 100pts.

A young German came for the room but only wants to pay 300 pts. I asked for 350; he said he would give an answer this evening. He is away all day which is a great advantage, but he said he might be called away at any time. I shall have to put an electric lamp in that room.

7pm. What a luxury to sit writing by electric light. The lodger came again to see the room and I said I would let him have it for 300 pts. He will give an answer this evening. Some of the present lodgers are a great help having plentiful rations and eating mostly at restaurants. Their landladies have the advantage of buying many groceries at cost price. This poor wretch – if he comes – is a clerk in a railway company, so has no advantages except that he would be away all day and that speaking no French I would be able to practise my German.

April 3rd. There are persistent rumours of peace. America is arming – a large number of Austrian soldiers with three guns and all their luggage on their backs went past our street this morning. They had come from across the water. [i.e. from the Asiatic side of the city].

April 6th. America has declared war on Germany; there is an atmosphere of future peace all around. I sent a note to Papa's namesake [Henry Newbolt], but he has taken no notice. I can't say that it is very polite of him. They are not under marching orders yet, but it is hourly expected that a break will come – the sooner the better if it has to come.

April 18th. I had meant to write about the prevalent sickness and to say that about ten days ago many have had it in our neighbourhood, and that some known people, especially doctors had died of it. Now the American ambassador has it. It is inoculated by a louse – horror! [presumably a bed-bug.] This morning I found one on my underclothing having first felt its bite, so if the wretched brute was a contaminated one, I may not see my dear ones after all. I am in God's hands – thy will be done dear Lord. What would become of Mama? I find no solution; she would find it very hard to change her habits. If in the course of 10–15 days I develop no symptoms of sickness, I will suppose that the wretched beast was not contaminated. I wonder where I caught it. Many people are afraid of trams and crowds but I have been in neither. The police are doing all they can in the way of disinfecting public places and taking up people who are not clean, but nevertheless the illness is spreading.

April 21st. America has been given notice to leave. I do not know how the ambassador will manage. We are to go to Holland for protection, [meaning the Dutch Legation] I know no details as yet. We felt pretty comfortable with America to back us. The Italians go to Spain as well as the Montenegrians. French, Russians and Americans to Sweden.

The '*Scorpion*' had been disarmed some days ago. [This was the British Embassy launch/yacht which had a cannon on board for firing ceremonial salutes; it had presumably been taken over by the US. Embassy]

Robert College [the US technical college on the European side of the Bosphorus at Bebek], will be taken – that is a nice haul.

Miss Harty is to be married before they go [presumably to an American] she has done well with herself as her father not being a gentleman and having a grocery, no Englishman would marry her. She is well-educated and not bad looking.

St George's Day [23rd April]. I hope England's patron saint will protect all his people and give them peace and victory soon.

24th. A week ago, the papers said that meat was to be sold at no more than 30 pts. I told my butcher about this, but he just laughed and said that the article must have been an April Fool's joke. The next day, all the butchers just stood at their doors, grinning at all the poor people who rushed from door to door, wanting to buy meat. I suppose that this is what can be called a strike. I went to one man who knew me and he having just two small bits I pounced on them paying at the (illegal) rate of 40 pts, and was delighted at my find.

May 1st. Tomorrow I am going to the Dutch Legation to be registered; I must have a photo, it is a nuisance to have to pay at least another 10 pts for one; the spare one I had from the *'vesika'* I sent to Alfred for Xmas and according to Tizza it afforded him great pleasure, so I was well-paid for it. The Americans did not ask for a photo. I am going to sell another canary; I am sorry for it is one of the new ones and I wanted it to welcome Alfred, but I need money and their food is getting quite an item; I feel half tempted to sell a couple but do not know if I will have the courage to undertake it.

May 4th. I feel downright miserable; without boasting I find that I have been very courageous but afraid that my courage is going fast. I still want to keep myself in hand, but at times my hands are weak. Very likely we will spend another winter like the last; we will by then be quite worn out morally and physically.

May 9th. War is hard enough on everybody. Miss Daleggio [?] who has a softening of the brain I think, goes round begging, after getting a piaster off me, attacked a poor Austrian soldier who was leaving St. Marie at the same time as me. The way the man prayed was sufficient to lift ones soul to God. As I passed him she was whispering to him in French. He tried to say he did not understand, and as I passed he beckoned to me. "Don't worry" I said, "She is not in great need, but is asking for alms". "I have none to give" he said, " I am a very poor man and have a wife and four children, I cannot help others, I come from Posan (or something like that) in the Tyrol, do you know my country – perhaps you have been there?" "I pity you" I said, "for I too have two sons fighting". "Thanks, thanks" he said and shook my hand. The poor man seemed in such need of sympathy. I joined in his prayers and asked God to grant his wishes, nothing more I suppose but that he should return to his home and family; he must be a poor peasant who has never left his hills before. Oh! this is a cruel war which will break many hearts.

May 12th. The fever scare has subsided, thank God. People say that cholera will be the next trouble; others talk of peace in two months, others two years. Meanwhile there are fearful battles going on. Mrs Budelglia [?] has had news of the serious illness of her youngest son and has left for Austria. She is lucky to be able to join him; we poor belligerent mothers have no such hope in case of need.

May 13th. We have had a very pleasant Spring, i.e. it has not been too hot, as I only go out in the morning or evening, I have only once been out without my fur tippet. I shall soon be shabby, which for the sake of my dear ones, I would not like. In the way of shoes I am already badly off. I have only one good pair, so that in case of need, I can look respectable, but my second pair is past mending. I do not believe that I have spent more than three pounds on myself since Alfred left, and that includes making myself a coat out of a skirt. I do not write this boastingly, but am happy to have managed so well. I have to keep the maid in slippers of course, made out of home materials and rope. I have increased her wages to 70 pts which is still very little. According to the papers, Salonika is likely to be abandoned; if so, where will my dear boys be sent? Not to France I hope. I should dread it.

May 15th. I told Harty [*] that I would not be able to pay him till the end of the month. He said "of course". I hope to sell a female canary. I have seven and will gladly get rid of them. I asked 25 pts; if I could sell two it would be a help. I lent the man a pretty good cage to take them away with, and now he would like to buy it. I was delighted and asked 50 pts. I wonder if he will pay it – it was rather risky; I would prefer 40 pts to nothing.

The man came for 58 pts. for the electricity, i.e. since I began on 20th March. Well, I could not do otherwise than ask Mama for a pound which she very willingly gave me. Now I have kept the rest [change] so will have a little money for a short while.

It seems they are fighting where our dear boys are.

21st. Yesterday I met Mrs Apikian who apologised for not coming to see us before going to the country [many people move out of the city for the Summer – either up the Bosphoros or to the islands in the Sea of Marmara], and asked me to go and spend a day with them – "it would please us all," she said. "I can't I said", and tears came to my eyes. [She could not leave her mother alone].

May 26th. I have just read the beginning of this journal and am amused at the idea of a loaf of bread at 6pts being something monstrous. I now pay 23 pts.

I have just had a great grief; our canaries have all died of hunger! Awful! Feeling limp these days, I had not been upstairs for three days but put the box of seed outside my door thinking she [i.e. the servant] would see it and remember to feed them, but somehow one thing or another came in the way, and when she did go up, she found all four dead. I was so pleased to think that Alfred should come home and find them well. It has upset me dreadfully. Only a week ago I refused to sell one.

Whit Monday. According to the papers, we are beaten everywhere – it is most disheartening. Maybe someone will tell me the contrary in the course of the day. I shall go for my last lesson to the Saveiro's. They are going to the country, so I will have nothing else coming in; what is to be done? One must grin and bear it.

1st June. Our wedding 30 years ago – a lifetime. I went out for a walk and met Miss Jacod [?]; I stopped her and we exchanged the latest news which suggests that only in January will hostilities cease after which there will be an armistice until April. I had to leave her for I could not talk. I shall get a reputation for crying when spoken to, but cannot help it. I put up with mother all day long, for she is full of her troubles and I cannot burden her with mine. Having to wait another six months seems beyond my power of endurance. If I could be assured that at the end of that time, they would all be alive and well, but every day ahead is one of danger. The landlady has the famous [?] fever and is not expected to live; her poor daughter will remain all alone. Her son took a holiday and was here for three weeks, then went back about a month ago.

June 8th. I have had 500 pts from Mr. Grancheroff [? a Bank official] and 300 from the British Relief, the last I am to have monthly so I feel I can manage until the end of June. Mrs Hazel [?] died this morning. Luckily her daughter is engaged, otherwise, poor thing she would be very lonely. Her eldest sister is in America and her brother is at the front.

June 9th. Coming back from church, I met Sylvia who said she was going to order her wood and charcoal for the winter. It will cost her Lts.30! If it cost me Lts.3, I could not afford it. She has more lessons than she can manage, but she deserves comfort, poor thing for she is bereft of all family affection. I would not change my life with hers for three times her comfort.

June 10th. Mr Kerastesgian [?] came to see Tizza's room. His wife is in Prinkipo [one of the islands in the Sea of Marmara, quite close to the city – now called Buyukada], so he wants a room for the weekdays only. I only asked 350 pts though I dreaded his coming as I heard that he is an awful fusser. He said he found the room nice, but we were out of the way. Now it seems he has taken a room at Mrs. [illegible]. I am not sorry; I would like the 350 pts, but I would hate to have a lodger.

I am worried about Mama; it seems she is getting worse. I have been living in dread for the last two years, but now she is really declining.

14th. We are becoming vegetarians. We have not eaten meat for ten days. I fancied that I could not possibly manage a bill of fare without meat, but I see it is possible. I do not think our health is suffering, but Catrina [the maid] is at last getting thinner. She was huge last winter; it was ugly.

June 19th. Having heard that our bishop gets messages sent to soldiers I went to the chancellery. One of his secretaries took down my messages which they would send through the Vatican – I wonder if they will get it. I hear that there has been a Zeppelin raid on London.

I do think it a little funny that Alfred does not find a way of enquiring how I manage. I will never mention that I have difficulty in making both ends meet, for I do not want him to worry poor fellow – but surely he cannot think that with the St.15 he authorizes me to take, I can live and pay St.7½ rent a month.

June 22nd. Yesterday, coming along the [illegible] we saw a ship full of soldiers, Turkish and German, the latter wearing khaki helmets and goggles. Poor things, how many will return to their homes?

28th. An order came out that rice was to be given out at 30 pts. [? an oke.] Whereas it was sold at 40 to 46 – immediately there was none to be had! That is always the result of a reduction in prices. I went to a shop to get 100 [?], telling him to weigh it out of one of the sacks he had on show, he refused, and as I insisted, he got in such a rage that he slipped and fell and spread all the rice on the floor. It was comical!

July 4th. Mama has been in bed for the last ten days and I have been near her night and day. She would not have a doctor, but I persuaded her to see Dr Kevack [?] who said that her heart is not bad, but her lungs were a bit lazy and gave her some medicine; he thinks it could be anaemia of the brain. She says she feels very bad and talks of death; she either gets cross or dozes all the time. After that, I insisted that she has Extreme Unction [The Catholic sacrament given to those near death].

Greece has declared war.

July 9th. Turkish women now do the road sweeping. I saw one wearing a quite decent black silk *feriye* [Moslem face-covering.] Poor things, they too are to be pitied.

During the night we had our first air fight. Of course we understood what it was though being Ramadan [the Moslem month of fasting – guns were fired to start and end the time of the fast] we do hear firing in the night. This however was quite different. All the lights were put out. At the theatre they had a gala night and must have fared rather badly when they came out. The damage is not known. [Apparently some Allied aircraft were based on some of the Greek islands closest to Turkey.] I thought Mama was better, but last night she alarmed me again. The troubles in Germany gives hope to some people.

Should Mama not get over her weakness, I shall let the flat and go as a governess. The Grancheroffs would be delighted to have me – it is a regular desert where they are and there is no church, but I would soon be able to make both ends meet. I do not want Alfred to return and find me full of debts.

22nd. Catrina was out for over two hours looking for rolls, and has come back with the cut of a whip on her forehead; very few were given out and there were fights.

July 27th. A letter from Tizza – what pleasure! It was only 20 days old. Alfred is evidently with the boys. I am sure that life suits him better than in London. [They were in Salonika]. I hope he is also getting good pay. Poor Tizza is alone, she only had one week's holiday which she spent in Baddow. [in Essex, with her aunt Sophia]. Since Xmas she works till 10½. I hope she gets an extra bonus for it.

July 29th. I feel very cross – Catrina [the maid] is an awful expense. She eats more than Mama and I put together. We managed to get a bit of beef which we made into koftes [*meat balls*]. She brought eleven to the table; I do not know if she kept any for herself. I gave Mama two, had three myself and she had six.

A German naval man was brought as a lodger [prospective] by Marie Pamaty [?]. He saw the room and liked it; Marie whispered that I should ask 5 pounds; I asked him four, but when I said we were English, he said he would not mind, but they had orders not to live with belligerents. I was not sorry; I cannot have lodgers with Mama ill; we both keep our rooms open and I go in and out in my night-gown. I cannot have a man to whom I would give a latch-key, coming in.

August 2nd. I must either have a good laugh or a cry. Here I am at the beginning of the month with no money and Harty's bill of 670 pts to pay plus all August's expenses to meet. Presently I will take my *'tourah'* brooch [a brooch with the sultan's emblem on it, presumably in gold] and see what I can get for it. I had been offered 220 pts. I went out with the brooch and a small gold coin and was offered 163 and by another 176. I met Mr. Descuffs [?] to whom I gave the pieces to see if he could get me a better price. I also answered an advertisment for English lessons to a German officer.

I must find my album of old Constantinople views, very old ones and find the address of some Germans who write on Constantinople architecture; perhaps they might buy them, but I cannot find them.

August 5th. There was a ring at the door, and there was Mr. Desnadino's [?] little boy with an American sailor. The latter wanted a room. I was rather staggered at first, but thought I would have to re-adjust my prejudices; well, he pays Lt.4 a month and sleeps here every 6 days. He brings no luggage and needs nothing. He paid straight away. If that is not providence, I don't know what is. Of course – he is a sailor, but he seems pleased with his room and with me. He gets his salary in gold and consequently it comes to only £1 to him. He even said that if the change gets higher, he will give me the difference – is that not generous! Maybe Tizza felt her dear mummy in such difficulty and asked the dear Lord to help.

August 7th. My sailor who went out at 5 pm saying he would be back in a couple of hours, but never turned up at all last night. I had made up my mind that having only one day ashore he would go out on the spree and was thinking that he might not find the door in the small hours of the morning. But then it struck me that being a belligerent, he could not be out after ten. He never turned up at all though I sat up till 11 and slept badly. This morning I did not go to church thinking he might call on his way on board. Anyway, I am in possession of Lt.4 and will wait further developments. I hope he has not been locked up. 9 pm – he did not turn up today and consequently will not till next Sunday. It is splendid.

The bank, after making me wait a week sent "Mrs Newbolt a loan of Lt.3". The idiots! I wrote and almost told them so. They take away the loan from me and give it to Mama.

August 10th. I got 322 pts for my gold pieces; I am sorry to have sacrificed the brooch for it would have gone to Tizza. I feel sure she would not begrudge it me. I may, one of these days get her a smaller one.

August 13th. Well. Of all the funny nights I have ever spent, last night was the funniest, and I never felt the need of my dear Alfred more. Our lodger came home just after lunch. I saw him coming up the hill. I said, "you do not enjoy your room very much". "I will be here all night this time" he replied. He went out at 3 and came back again about 5. I opened the door to him, but did not speak as Père Appolinaire had just come. His door being closed, I surmised that he was asleep, but would get up later to go out for dinner. After my snack I wondered what to do to wake him up, for if he went out too late he would find nothing to eat. At 9, I went to his door and knocked, no answer, then harder and then quite hard. I then ventured to open the door, but found it locked. At 10½ I went to bed with a skirt and jacket ready to put on. At 1am I heard a big commotion; his door opened and I heard him talking. I thought at first that he must be ill, but had not the courage to go to his door. He then rambled on chuckling to himself; I presumed he was drunk and was very frightened, then he got up, chucked water about, moved tables and chairs. He moved about the rooms; I did not see him properly, but think he had bare arms and legs; he went back into his room, made a big noise and then banged his door to. I then slept, dressed as I was.

Catrina, hearing all the noise had barricaded herself in. At 6½ he
came out. I was in the dining room, looked out and answered his
"good day Madam", but did not have the pluck to speak to him.
Now I don't know what to do! I shall be afraid if he comes back
next Saturday – he must have brought a bottle back with him and
drunk it all afternoon. Catrina says he chucked a bottle out of the
window onto the waste ground.

August 17th. That four pounds was a present for my birthday [15th
August – her 'feast day'.] Our sailor wrote saying he was not
allowed to leave the ship and would not keep the room. I suppose
he was ashamed of himself; it is better so. I now must look out for
someone else.

One of my visitors wished me 'another fifty years', I said "God
forbid" – old age is a purgatory on earth, and being such is not
pleasant. When feeling my end, I should like to be like to do like
the elephants do and go somewhere and die. [She died aged 100 in
Surbiton, Surrey.]

It was the new Austrian emperor's birthday. (Funny that it
should be one day sooner than the old one.) At the reception, the
ambassador said that we were in for another winter campaign. Our
good father the Pope is acting as a mediator; will God grant him
the fulfilment of his wishes? Mama is fidgety and keeps telling me
of the servant's imperfections, which she exaggerates – all this
seems so trivial compared to the idea of Peace, Peace, Peace!

August 19th. Dear Alfred's birthday. God bless him and keep him
safe in body and soul. It is nice that the dear boys are near him. I
wonder if he has congenial work and if he is well-paid. Our friends
are fighting splendidly by all I can ascertain

All the rents in the house have been raised 3/11 liras a month,
but not mine. I met Miss Hazel [?] just before her marriage and she
said that she had had to raise all the rents, "but not yours Mrs
Lyster, not yours, only do not tell the others". I call this
providential; why should she not raise mine?

Volume 2, August 1917

August 23rd. I shall have to put electricity in the kitchen, in Mama's room and the spare room in the hope of letting the latter. Someone was saying that none of my three dear ones need have left; that even if Alfred had been deported, he would have found a way of not being away too long; that Freddie would have found work and that Tizza would have been a comfort and a help as she could have got into the Consulate or the US Embassy like the other girls and got good pay – those who were paid Lts.12, now get four times as much; this time they will get 51, as the pound is 425 pts.

[My father, her eldest son, Henry, was already in England when the war started. I presume that the other 'three dear ones' left at the beginning of the war, but have no facts to base this surmise on. Her mother 'Mama' fell and broke a leg (or a hip) just before they were planning to leave, making a sea voyage impractical, hence their stay in Turkey, and this diary].

I did not agree with my friend; it would have been a very cramped life for all, particularly for the children.

29th. I have made up my mind to pay Lts.10½ for three electric fixtures as I must let a room having nothing else to sell, so I must exert myself to let a room. I cannot find the photo albums and now have only Tizza's paints to sell. I have told one or two people [about them], we will see what they will fetch.

31st. I wish my dear Alfred were here. I am not a business woman. It seems to me that engaging myself to pay Lts.10½ is madness on my small means. We have no wood. I have no boots, no stockings, no vests, no galoshes and here am I undertaking to pay this sum in two lots. Lts.7 now and 3½ next month.

September 7th. What an accident or rather calamity. The whole of Haydar Pasha Station has been blown up. [This was/is the main-line station on the Asiatic side of the city, connecting the rest of the Ottoman Empire with the capital. It was the start of the Baghdad railway built by the Germans]. The first explosion was terrific with many panes of glass even broken in our street. Neither Mama or I were frightened however, as we could see from our window that it was across the water [the Sea of Marmara], but those who did not know what the explosion was and where it took place, were beside themselves – I can quite understand it. There are it seems very many victims. I hope it will stop the projected campaign. It seems that not a pane of glass is to be found whole, and there are none in the market to replace them. There are very many victims, many were projected into the sea and dead soldiers are being washed ashore. It seems the mishap was the result of an accident, but of course everyone has a different tale to tell.

[My father had added a note to this entry – "This calamity for the Turks was done by some of our agents who placed bombs in the railway yard full of ammunition to be used against General Allenby's advance in Palestine. It was still in ruins when we entered the place as victors". I do not know if this comment as to the action of 'agents' is born out by any official enquiry.]

September 18th. I began my lessons with little Saviero again. It will mean Lt.1½ more a month. I have had any amount of applicants for English lessons in answer to Mr. Grancheroff's advertisement which being very stupidly worded brought me a whole lot of people who wanted to give private lessons. Only one girl wants to come. I told her to be here on Friday when husband and wife are coming. The difficulty will be to get them permission to travel. He said he could manage it, but I doubt it.

The great news is that we are to have a bigger ration of bread. There is great excitement about it. We get 110 gms more a head and pay 10 paras more for it.

We have had the electric man in today; he made the place an awful mess. Thereupon a German came to see the room. I asked him four pounds; he said he would give me an answer by Saturday.

The people where he is now living sent him, and say that he is quiet and tidy.

19th. I have sent a message to Henry via the Red Crescent. [The Moslem equivalent of the Red Cross.] I wonder if he will get it. This is about the fifth, but I have not had one single reply.

September 22nd. The lodger has not given an answer which means that he will not come. We will not have light for another ten days, so if I found a lodger, I would be perplexed how to light his room. I have to appear before a committee on Wednesday which is rather humiliating to be seen amongst all the relief crowd, but since beggars cannot be choosers, must accept things as they come.

October 1st. I have a lodger! A cheap one, only Lts.3, but he is young and can't pay more. I thought of my dear boys so I said 'come'. He is working in the German Military Hospital. He went out to look for lodgings, asking at all doors where he saw electricity. Of course he liked the room and says he will bring some things cheap, we shall see. He is a mere boy, will be 21 in May and seems a gentleman though he is only a soldier. I love all young people, both girls and boys. God bless them all be they German or English. He is an only child, and his mother is a widow.

October 3rd. I was led away being in a soft mood. I am told that I let him have the room too cheap. As long as no-one else turns up, it is alright. Anyway [his] 10 pts a day will pay for bread. He brought petroleum the first night, and we filled a lamp as we have not had the current through yet. Some of these fellows bring many things home for which they make [their] people pay very little. I will go to the electricity company to sign the new contract for the kitchen.

October 6th. My poor diary is my best friend – I cannot tell my worries to anyone. I classify my friends according to their tendencies. To Sylvia I can tell my domestic worries – to Clementine talk about Mama, to Nina go deeper into financial difficulties, but I rarely see her alone. My own true feelings I express to no-one except our dear Lord and this diary.

October 7th. I went to the German mass. The Father who preached said that we must all pray for peace, but not that they should become slaves to the English. What is our dear Lord to do? Both sides very probably pray equally well.

I have five ways of getting news of my loved ones, and yet I am without any. The Dutch Consulate, the Vatican, the Red Cross, Mr Hodley [?] and Virginie. [There are several references to this last person, but I do not know who she is].

October 10th. The reason why the electric co. do not send someone to fix up our light is that the German S [?] is coming and they are all up to their necks in work. It seems that the Germans have received orders not to spread Willie's [presumably Kaiser Willheim's] arrival, but we hear that he is expected Monday. They also say – but there are always a lot of 'says', that all belligerents will not be allowed out of doors for three days, i.e. during his stay. I suppose it does not apply to women.

(No date). The Emperor is here. I have not seen him; his friends, or rather allies have given him a showy welcome. All the front rooms of the belligerents' houses have been sealed up, and a whole lot of people have been shipped out to Prinkipo for a few days. I do not suppose that they mind as it is ideal weather. My soldier is leaving tomorrow. He has been as stingy as they make them in their country; if he had not gone, I should have turned him out. What a difference with my American sailor. I have found a new way of writing – through Madrid, but will I get an answer?

October 18th. Willie [the Kaiser] is going, or has gone; the two other allies will also come. Two days ago, all the belligerent priests of the parish churches got orders to abstain from their ministry in every form. Today it seems, the order was cancelled. – Why? A dentist friend of our last lodger came to see the room. I asked him Lts.4 and some provisions at cost price, but stupid like, I did not close with him and now regret it. He wants neither breakfast nor anything else. The vice-consul would give Lts.7, but then it would mean minding our p's and q's all the time – he is too grand for us. If I could get him for French conversational classes, it would be grand, say Lts.2 for three hours a week. I shall go to see Père Denis tomorrow. He is leaving for Rome and I will ask him to write to Tizza and Alfred telling them to write [to me] through the Vatican, giving them proper addresses.

Having answered three advertisements and expecting one other lodger, I must stay at home all day which is a nuisance.

Today I thought that Father Dyoinsius [?] was leaving for Rome as Secretary to Bishop Papadopoulos who is going to be the Head of the Oriental Department at the Vatican. I went to see him, but he was not in, so I have written to him asking him to write to Alfred and Tizza. I do all I can to keep in touch with my dear ones, but all to no avail.

October 20th. The dentist has not come; it is a pity. A Turk came who wanted to live in an English family so as to learn the language, but he thought that Lts.4 for the room and Lts.2 for an hour's conversation five times a week, tremendous. All the telephones have been taken away from the belligerents' houses and offices.

I know the dear Lord is very good, but why should he spare me rather than thousands of other mothers who pray for their own dear ones, very likely much better than I do. Poor Mrs [?], who had only one son and who is such a good Christian and prayed to God so much to spare her son, and yet He thought fit to take him – His will be done, in happiness and in sorrow.

October 23rd. Coming back from shopping, I met Mrs de Wodsky [?] who came with me and had her pocket picked whilst she was buying vegetables. Of course it was not my fault, but if she had been alone, she may have had her wits more about her. I lent her some money to pay for what she had bought, and coming to return it an hour later she asked me if I would not hire out my piano as she had some friends who would pay me Lts.2 for it. I said Yes, as I knew nothing about hiring pianos. She said her friends would send for it in the afternoon as she was going there for lunch. When she left, I went to the Ferra's [?] and told them. They said that pianos were hired out at Lts.4 a month as there were none to be had. I was very much perplexed. When the men came for the piano, I gave the servant who came with them a note telling Mrs de. W. what I had been told. I ought to have warned them in time. I suppose she will be cross with me, but then she ought to have known that Lts.2 was very little to offer. Anyway, I feel very uncomfortable, and I wish I could clear up this business. Miss Armas [?] informed me that small pianos are let out to private houses for Lts.2½. If the wretched woman had given me time to think, I would have asked three pounds and might have had them, but asking four, I got nothing, and have acted badly – business ought never to be done in a hurry.

24th. I spent my time trying to mend or rather patch, an old pair of stockings of Freddie's, about ten years old I suppose; another of Tizza's brought from England six years ago. I did not feel much scruple [sic] about making use of them for I am certain they would not object. With two pairs patched I will at least be warm; if I had boots to wear, I would not mind the patches, but with shoes I am afraid they might show.

Electricity was given to us for the kitchen, Mama's room and Tizza's – the latter looks so nice lighted [sic] up, but it saddened me to have the cage without my little bird in it.

Mrs de W. did not turn up which means that she is cross with me. I am really sorry, but I do not feel inclined to give our piano.

October 25th. A young fellow came who wanted the room with the piano put in it for Lts.5, but I did not fancy him and refused. Today I have let the room for Lts.7. It is the utmost the room could fetch, but I had to put a second bed in it, and take all my little girl's things out. We seemed to have fallen very low – first a sailor, then a soldier and now actors! An agent asked if I would take a husband and wife, I said No, then he said he had two actors, I said No to that, then he said he suggested the secretary and scenic manager of the Viennese troupe that arrived yesterday and as he accepted that they should pay Lts.7, I thought I had better close in with the offer; then they came, liked the room immensely. I gave them 2 keys, but they want two more.

October 28th. Our lodgers are splendid so far. God has been very good to me; I could not possibly have done better. True I had to pay 7 *mejidies* [a 20-piastre piece] to the agent who brought them; it was preposterous, but he said that he had told me it was 20%. I had understood him to say it was 20 [? piastres] per head. Anyway, it is only so much of the first month's rent, and they will remain until April. I was able to pay the electricity, and I paid Harty over 300 pts I owed from my old account. Yesterday I got [?] from the British Relief, so I do feel grateful to the dear Lord. My room is like a pigsty as I have had to turn out all Tizza's drawers to give room to the lodgers.

The news from Italy are [sic] bad; they seemed to have lost all they gained with such difficulty. [This must be a reference to the Battle of Caporetta where the combined Axis broke the Italian line.] I hope it may not be as bad as the papers here make out. There has been firing of guns in the distance since the morning, and three aeroplanes passed just now, but it is only practice I suppose.

October 29th. All Pera [the main European quarter] was beflagged. Poor Italy is in a bad way.

November 2nd. Our lodger is splendid – he leaves at 9am and comes home at quarter past one the next morning. He makes no noise, and is besides quite a nice fellow – almost a gentleman [!]. He is married and has a little boy aged five. He was a soldier for two years, and is still under military rule, but I do not know yet what his ordinary calling is. He says life in Vienna is quite cheap, though there are restrictions.

November 6th. I went to the Dutch Legation and was shown two communications from Alfred. One dated March, and the other June. He says he has a good situation as cashier 'here', but where 'here' is, I do not understand. [In fact, he and his two sons were all based in Salonika: see photograph no. 5.] He says that he sees the two boys who are together, once a month, and that Tizza writes once a month and has every comfort. God bless them all four. Who would have thought that I alive, Alfred and the boys together and Edythe [Tizza] all alone in England; also that the boys would be doing the same kind of work.

November 9th. I am very much perplexed. A German lady who is employed in an office, came to see the dining-room; she did not like it, but when she saw Tizza's room she fell in love with it and suggested that I should tell my lodgers to take the front room, so I told them that I had thought of turning the dining room into a bedroom, offering it to them. They jumped at it and said that they would look out for a lodger for their room. This afternoon, one of them brought a lady, of course one of their troupe. She seemed all right, and he guaranteed her, but I still thought she was very plainly dressed – the idea of turning our flat into a lodging house for actors, is not pleasing to me, so tomorrow I must say that I have found someone else, and I must send word to the other woman. If she will pay for English conversation besides the rent for the room, I will take her, but if she thinks she is going to run after me and speak English gratis, she can look elsewhere. Meanwhile, when I think of all the work needed to turn the dining room into a bedroom, and my room into a jungle, I feel bad.

November 13th. I have sold some more things; clothes of Freddie and Alfred. I shall have to go on selling clothes until I get out of debt and get in a little wood for the winter. No one has come for the room; I am going to advertise it. I heard this evening that the Jews' capital had fallen [presumably Jerusalem.] It is a long stretch since the last crusade.

November 14th. I am in one of my miserable moods today; I was told by the bank that I might have a part of the groceries given to us, maybe next Saturday; this will be a great help, but what will we do until then? Prices go up every day. My one idea is to make money. Yesterday I sold some bits of lead [?] which Freddie had collected. I do need to let the piano and the dining room.

November 23rd. All our provisions are now in – it is a pleasant feeling; we also have charcoal and light, unless we as belligerents are cut off, but I do not believe this rumour. On the 28th, I suppose that our lodgers will pay their rent. I will call at the Dutch Legation to see if there is any message – in another month we will have Xmas; will it be the last spent apart? About a dozen lodgers have been to see our dining room, but I have closed with no-one. One Austrian vice-consul would pay Lts.8, but he wanted the use of the sitting room after 6pm, and two more electric lamps, besides the nuisance.

November 24th. Mrs [?] says she has a lodger who will pay Lts.6 for our dining room, but I must have it in order for him to see it – I understand one cannot buy a pig in a poke, but still moving all my things out of my drawers, and putting them where? is a great deal of work. I shall move the sideboard and dining table into my room. God grant that I should soon move them back again. I am tired of being alone; my brain aches sometimes from planning one thing and another. I only go to Mama for the minor part of my troubles, for it is no good worrying her; she has nothing but her aches and pains to think about. The actors have asked to pay less for their room; I said No, but would regret to lose them and their Lts.7. They never come home before 1.15 am; we hear them, but they do not disturb us. If they really cannot pay, I shall not risk losing them, and will take Lts.6. Good night all my dear ones; where are you, and what are you doing?

November 29th. Yesterday we worked like niggers [!], and turned the dining room into a splendid bedroom. I miss my nice dining room, but I am happy to find the means to increase my income. A lady came to see the room and liked it very much, she did not have the authority to rent it for her cousin, an officer; she said she would write and tell him.

Russia has asked for peace; some people think a lot may come about through this. I suppose that the party who want peace will be overruled by those who want to go on fighting and whose interests are at stake if the plans they have laid do not mature.

December 8th. Our room has been let for Lts.6 plus Lt.1 for cooking his breakfast. We have not had such a fall of snow for some time. Russia is negotiating for peace with her old enemies. We do not yet know what our people will do.

December 11th. I cannot live in this cold weather. I am dressed like an onion. Thank God, I have enough to put on except stockings. I have however, put on my old mended pair. There is a ten-day truce between Russia and Germany and her allies of course.

December 15th. Our two actors have gone; I regret their 7 pounds and their being away at bedtime, but otherwise they were not very desirable. They took with them our hat brush and a Japanese box of Tizza's! [?]. Mama is not very well; I am afraid for her for she has taken to her bed and cannot see to read so that life is very slow and sad for her. Our lodger has moved into Tizza's room; he prefers it and as he is a very clean man, it suits me too, but I do hope to let the dining room again.

December 18th. Today week it will be Christmas. I do hope my dear ones are well and will spend it joyfully. Russia is coming to terms with Germany. Of course I regret it as it will make things easier for our enemies, but it may be a means of the world coming to some sort of agreement. Père Louis, a Belgian, came to see Mama. He is very nice; I showed him our room and he said he knew of a German doctor who might be interested. I had seen him walking up our road, and had thought how I would have liked him as a lodger. Should this thing succeed, I would again have to thank St. Anthony for I had knelt before his statue. If the doctor does not come, I will bear him [St. Anthony], no grudge. We would be delighted to have him in the house; he is about 40 and seems very nice. He now lives at Tokatlians [one of the smart hotels], so will he like our plain furniture?

December 20th. We are very near Xmas; how miserable this one will be. Last year I had news; this year there seems no likelihood of any. Switzerland is useless. I wrote a card a few days ago, but I have no hopes of it reaching them. They too must be anxious about us. I have no doubt that they will all think of poor me tomorrow for my birthday. I would not like to live too long and be a burden to any one. The Armistice with Russia has been signed; opinions are divided; our opponents all say we will have peace in a couple of months; we say that we fear it will begin all over again.

December 21st. My 53rd birthday – not a very bright one. Not a soul has thought of it, not even Mama – all the better! It would have saddened me still more. It seems that I am getting fat! Everyone tells me so. It is not due to over-indulgence, nor yet happiness, but to the fact that after 10.30 am. I hardly move from my seat. I now never go for a walk. All the better that my dear ones, if they are ever to see me again should not find me looking like a scarecrow. Our lodger said he would bring someone to see the room this afternoon. I hope he will take it and pay me in advance, for I am again hard up.

I am very cross with the maid just now. I sent her to Harty's to get some eggs thinking a trip out would stretch her legs a bit, and told her to choose big ones. If they are a good size, then one is enough for my supper (no afternoon tea), with camomile tea, otherwise I need two. Amongst the four she brought back, one was quite tiny! I was very much put out.

Christmas Eve. What memories this time brings to me. When the children were small, what a treat and what a feeling of being grown-up when they were allowed to go to Midnight Mass with us. Once we put Freddie to bed and promised to wake him up, but he seemed to be sleeping so well that we let him sleep till the morning.

He was furious with us, dear little man. What pleasure it was for us to pack up their little presents. When Henry was at home, getting the manger ready as well as the tree was his department. Tizza used to want to help too, but was not wanted. Most of the presents were trifles, but how they enjoyed opening their parcels. Where are they now? I have had no news since June. I shall go to bed now and hope to dream of my dear ones. This is the fourth year the children, i.e. the two [Edythe/Tizza and Freddie] have been away from home. Alfred left in January [?1915]. I wonder if my memory is fading from their minds. I am hungering for a kiss from their dear lips.

Xmas Day. Went to church and to holy communion. Unluckily I was not back when Father Cyril brought holy communion for Mama. Mrs Ferri [?] sent us some delicious cake and biscuits. Mr Ladiye [?], our only visitor brought me six little biscuits, being some that his German lodgers had given him; it was kind of him, but he had them in a piece of soiled newspaper which he brought out of his pocket; the look of them was not appetising, so I had them toasted and will eat them tomorrow – I hope the fire will have rid them of all impurities.

December 30th. It is settled; our dining room is let. The young fellow will come tomorrow; he seems very nice. I fancy he will be generous with his provisions. Mr Flamman [?] is also very nice, both lodgers being gentlemen. I hope to start the year well, but I owe money to everyone. It would be nice to start the month without arrears. All the Germans say that we will have peace in three months. Our people do not see things the same. How too delightful if we had peace soon and with good conditions – if not I prefer to wait. I must say that I have not come across a single G. who seems to have a hatred against us. It seems to me that they are more tolerant than we are.

I will have a holiday from my [English] lesson with the Saviero's for which I am pleased as they are not very interesting.

1918

January 2nd 1918. Here we are beginning a new year. I spent a pleasant day yesterday as Mama was in a better temper, which goes a long way towards making me happy too. Our new lodger came in on the 31st. His name is Natolsky [?]. He is a *chemiste* [? shirt-maker], not a chemist. He wears military clothes mostly, but not always. He gave me a packet of tea as a present, so now on my lodger's score I am satisfied, then I received Lts.6 Xmas present from the bank, it was a nice surprise. It seems as if the [British] Relief will be increased also, so I might be able to manage without borrowing any more. My new lodger is young and jolly, and I love youth for my own dear children's sake.

Père Denis with some friends, came with some sweets for Mama and some sausages for me, both bought with the best good will at the last moment at the first shop on the way; consequently bad, though he gave good money for them, we could eat neither. But still it was a pleasant day.

January 19th. I have not written for ages as I have no writing table; it being bitterly cold, I was not able to stay in my room to write on the sideboard, which I am doing now as the weather is glorious. My window is open and the sun is delightful.

Another reason to make me enjoy everything today is that I had good news from Alfred through Holland. The message was dated Nov. 9th, but still I am content. He is now Lieutenant Command Paymaster. I suppose he wears uniform. Evidently Henry is near him, but not my little Freddie, for Alfred says he sees the former very often and hear weekly from the latter as well as from Tizza who is in good hands and is working. Where can Freddie be? He will be 21 in a few weeks – a man. Alfred will look nice in uniform; who would have thought that he would come to the army again. He says he cannot send me more than the Stg. 22 through the bank. I need more than double! Mr N. [the lodger] has begun English lessons, so that I shall be at least 1½ pounds richer; then I have some of their washing done in the house so that I get another pound out of that, though I have increased the servant's wages by one pound – I would like another lesson. Everyone lets rooms; it is quite the go [sic].

27th. Our new lodger is making love or [? for] fun [?] to the dressmaker next door. I don't know how to act, and to whom to ask for advice. I dislike things of that sort. I was thinking I would have to borrow again to last the month when Mrs[?] came with the piano money for January and February, so now I can pay Harty's account before the end of the month.

God be praised, the famous *'Breslau'* has foundered [on the 20th] and it seems the *'Göben'* is in a bad way, though it is not admitted by its friends. We also lost one or two boats, the HMS *'Raglan'* [?] amongst smaller ones. I hope none of Arthur's boys were on board. [see p. 5].

February 1st. I have had a communication from the Vatican to the effect that Freddie and his brother are both well. His regiment was given, but not where the message came from, but having been sent as recently as Dec. 8th, I presume that Henry has joined Freddie in Italy? Our two lodgers are quite nice, but Mr. Flamman is very stingy, but as long as he pays all he owes, it does not affect me. He gives Catrina 20 pts a month whereas Mr. Natolsky gives her 50 – it is true that the latter often has his evening meal at home and we make him tea. Two days ago he brought me a *Times*! I was quite overcome, when I handled it, it seemed like seeing an old friend; of course it is forbidden – telling him I would keep it to enable him to read it at his lesson, I kept it 24 hours and was able to let Sylvia and Mr Harty enjoy it for a few hours. I saw nothing very new except that the Prince of Wales was with the [?] in Italy, but even the advertisements were pleasant reading. Nevertheless, when I came to casualties, I hesitated about looking at the list – thank God, there was nothing about any of ours. A Captain Newbold had been killed. I like giving my lessons to Mr. Natolsky; he is a very nice fellow.

February 12th. Peace has been signed with Russia; I wonder if it will help our enemies. Though the news is official, there have been no flags put up.

February 13th. The place IS [now] beflagged, but it seems to me a very funny peace; more like an armistice and nothing more. People are expecting prices to drop, but so far, things are stationary. How we manage to stay in good health is a wonder. There was a question of adding 25% to our salaries, but it fell through, only the actual clerks got it, plus 50% they had already[?].

March 2nd. I rarely write in my diary now, as having the two extra rooms, I have to help in the kitchen or with the dusting so that the house should be in good order. It seems that Russia and Germany are coming to terms and Roumania will have to do likewise. Our lodgers boast of having been called in to help the peace-loving element against their warlike brethren. Last night Mr Flamman who had seen an English *Times*, told me that "England too has had to restrict herself as to food". Yes, but two years after their enemies! [Meat and butter were rationed in London and

Southern England on 25 February].

The papers here talk of trouble in Ireland. I hope it is not true. The fact is that we hope to win through trouble in the enemies' camp, and they hope for exactly the same thing. Mr [?] is getting worried about Russia's defection. He always brought Russia's millions [men] as an invincible factor.

Both our lodgers are very satisfactory, and I look forward to my lesson evenings. My pupil has brought me two 'Times'. I will read them this evening, and am looking forward to the treat. After lunch I shall go to the bank to collect my Lts.13. I am again hard up this month; I must find some more things to sell so as to start clear next month.

March 9th. My baby's birthday. He is 21 today. God bless him as well as my big boy who was 30 on the 6th. China has joined Japan against the Russians; serve them right; but they [the Russians] are more to be pitied than blamed. I think it must be dreadful to be dismembered as is the case with them. I wonder where and how the boys spent their birthdays. I prayed for them, as that was all I could do.

March 15th. Mr Natolsky talked about going; i.e. leaving Constantinople, so that I thought I would have to start lodger hunting again, but things did not turn out as he wished. Giving his health as an excuse, the doctors ordered him to go to hospital. He has a catarrh of the throat, but it stands to reason as all day he wears a starched collar, then an awful military collar, so that his neck has over an inch of thick protection round it, then he used to come home, change into mufti with a single collar turned down only at the tips, then go out without a muffler. I will miss him. Before leaving he gave me some provisions. I enjoyed our lesson evenings, perhaps more than he did.

March 19th. The last of my seven artificial teeth has dropped off. It is very ugly but I dare not think of going to a dentist. Luckily I eat alone, for I always eat like a bunny (the children said), but now will do so more than ever.

The porter brought an Austrian soldier who was looking out

for a room for his officer. It was always my dream to have an Austrian officer. He asked if there was a piano; anyway he said he would tell his officer – I wonder if he will come. I must not be ungrateful however; no-one could be nicer than Mr. Natolsky.

The piano money is also very unsatisfactory; this month I have not been paid yet. I have sold Tizza's paints for 180 pts, but will only be paid for them at the end of the month. Miss [?] refused them saying they were too dry, but I thought that if I wait for Tizza's return, they will be dryer still. I had a photo stand (awful thing which I won at a lottery), and asked Mr. Wright [?] if he would try to sell it at the *Bon Marché* [?]; he marked it at 175, but it has not sold. I also want to dispose of Tizza's nurse's uniform [I do not think my aunt was ever a nurse – possibly a child's costume or fancy dress outfit,] I am told I could get a good price as linen is scarce.

March 27th. What heart-rending news. We were two years in taking what they took a first time in a few days, and now they have undone in three days what was retaken after such fighting. They will try for Calais and then will bombard England with their P26 [?] gun. We all feel rather ashamed and depressed. My Germans hope we will cry for mercy, if not, war will last another 2 years. I feel confident that dear England will never sue for peace. I still hope that we will turn the tables on them. I had a message from Alfred, he says that all four are well.

[This news must refer to the *Kaiser Schlact* offensive which had started a few days earlier whereby the German High Command, realising that with the reinforcements of US troops due to land in Europe shortly, they would have to make a serious push for Paris before the 'doughboys' arrived. At first it was very successful, dividing the allies, with the French defending Paris and the British, Calais, but the German logistic chain failed to keep up with the advance, it gradually began to peter out and a slow retreat followed].

I had to go and see about my teeth – he asked 20 Lts! I said that it was out of the question, and was going when he said that he would do the work and that I could pay what I liked – that occasionally one had to work for one's soul! I am going to get the plate tomorrow and wonder if Lts.6 would be decent payment – I would not like to pay more..

Mr Natolsky is back from hospital; he will not leave before the 20th April, and says he thinks he has someone who will take his room.

April 5th. The news does not seem to improve. We have stopped them, but I suppose they will break out somewhere else. Mr Natolsky now leaves tomorrow. Some other officer is coming so that I have no anxiety on that score. I wonder if he will be as nice; this one is really charming and I am quite fond of him. He is a Jew! I thought so from the first; why I do not know, but when he filled-up a police form he gave his religion as 'Mosaic' [?], so I never spoke of religion to him during our lessons, but on Saturday he called me into his room to give me a packet of honey, some biscuits and then some Jew's bread to taste which he had just received, and thereupon he spoke of Jewish traditions taking it for granted that I knew he was a Jew. He said he was a free-thinker as to religion, but took great interest in his race of which he seemed proud. He gave me some carbolic and [?] powder as well as a new reel of cotton. Mr Flamman I see less of. He is stingy, but of course he has a wife and two children which makes a difference.

April 8th. Our new lodger came yesterday. I never met anyone so full of conceit – if pricked he would burst! He told me more than once in a half hour's conversation that he was chief of the whole office, that he was above Mr Natolsky, that he had been chosen to take up this office because of his capacity; that his influence was felt even in Asia etc. etc. He wears an eyeglass! It is not because he does not wish to speak French, but because he can't speak it at all. He does not understand what I tell him; he wants to learn I suppose and speaks half French and half German. He says he has lots of clothes and stayed in his room all evening putting them away. He may be all right, but I think he will be an awful chatterbox which takes up my time and puts Mama out.

April 12th. I have seen very little of my lodger since the first day; he leaves everything open; I must see if I can get any groceries from him; he gave me a half-smoked tongue which we had to boil for two hours – I shall charge him for the charcoal. Mama is not very well. I went to Dr [?] who gave me a prescription. I was asked 75 pts for it, so only had half made up. The Ferris are going to the country for six months. She is very run-down and needs a change. I shall miss her terribly for she is an ideal neighbour, and I always feel safer about Mama knowing I could go to her for advice, and if necessary, help. Now she is going away; it is a cross which I will have to bear. Dr Bernhardt [the new lodger]said that if the English Army had German officers they would conquer the world. He thinks very highly of the English soldiers, but not so of the officers.

April 15th. It seems just now that the Bulgarians and the Turks do not hit it off and there may be a little unpleasantness between Austria and Germany over the L.C. incident [?] – they are always looking for rents in our armour. Our lodger has his evening meal in his room; tea, eggs, boiled tongue etc. I must see about his paying me the fortnight ahead.

I had three chances of finding money today; one Lts.1½ from the *Bon Marché* for the photo-stand I had left there; 1½ from the Savaiero's for my lesson and then money for the piano which had been owing since the 1st.

April 16th. Last night I had a note from the D.L. [Dutch Legation] telling me I had to go for a communication. It was dated the 9th. I was delighted to get news from Alfred, but hoped to hear direct from Tizza. However, Alfred says she is all right and writes to him regularly. He mentions again that I may take Lts.30 from the bank if necessary, and that Henry is a full lieutenant now – I had hoped he would be a captain by now. Alfred says that they are both in safe posts, not in any danger. He again says he will be home in August. He had received my messages of Aug. and Oct. this morning.

I was in desperate straits for money and had to borrow again. Tomorrow I should get 715 pts from the relief, and then maybe I will sell Tizza's serge dress and Freddie's dress suit for 500 pts. I might have found more, but the thing is to find just the people who need such things.

April 24th. It seems the English and French are at liberty to leave Turkey – the men after 50 and boys before 15 and all women; there has been talk about it for some time, but at last the order is out. My heart aches to go and join my dear ones, but of course I cannot leave Mama; anyway, what would I do with our flat? Let it to people who might leave in a few months? If I left it to strangers, we might find nothing on our return, but I must say that the open door tempts me terribly. I must find out about the permission for departure – it seems a ship will meet them at Smyrna [Izmir].

A shark was caught near [?], and was being sold at 40pts an *oke* in the fish market – it looked lovely and a lot of people were buying it. Those 5 pts I paid for my teeth have handicapped me terribly.

Going to the D.L. today to send a message to Alfred thanking him for the 8 pounds extra he allows me, I found a message from Tizza. Poor Darling, she never got one of my messages, only the one I sent to Arthur [?], to which she was answering. Anyway, now I have her address. She says she is well, but is working, which means she does it because she has to, but under present circumstances, she cannot idle her time away. She says the lady [Mrs Stack] she is living with is nice to her, which is a great happiness to me. I immediately answered to her address and hope to get an answer in about two months.

Volume 3, May 1918

May 1st. I went to Harty's for eggs; 4 for 14 pts. His son is still shut up, but his mother who went to see him, waited outside and had a few lines from him saying he was well. I hope the poor boy will soon be let out, for he is certainly not guilty [?] I am happy Freddie is away.

May 7th. Dr Kerouk [?] came to see about my inflamed ear; I look an awful sight; my face is all out of shape – my dear ones would laugh if they could see me. He also examined my heart, and as I expected, he prescribed digitalis, also iron chloroform. He had the kindness to stamp the prescription from the British Relief, so that I will have nothing to pay. I am so pleased to be English. God bless dear England.

May 12th. Last night, Mr Flamman came in and gave me a copy of 'Le Soir'. The leader was something about peace; the other papers also talk of peace, but I do not feel it.

May 15th. It is quite a settled thing that the English and French should leave. The men after 60, and boys before 17; the women are free. There is great excitement in both colonies. I went for my British Relief money today. The other day, I had the courage to steal! Yes, I stole two small pieces of sugar from our officer lodger. I felt such an overwhelming wish for something sweet that I went into his room and took out two small lumps which I ate. I believed the bank was going to give us some sugar, but it was only for the clerks who are in active service, so I am unable to buy any to replace my theft as I hoped to do. I was ashamed to have to confess it, it seemed so mean.

May 18th. Tomorrow the Austrian Emperor and his wife are expected. I suppose they will go past our street on account of the three houses occupied by Austrian soldiers. I had a communication from Alfred via the Vatican dated 9th March, saying all are well.

Whit Monday – I am off my head with worry. Yesterday our new landlord came to say that he wants the flat! What a blow to me! What shall I do? Who will advise me? He said the sooner I could let him have it, the better. I told him I could not give an answer before September, our contract being up on 1st October. Were I alone, I would sell everything and leave. I shall try to let things shape themselves for a month at least (but can I?). I fear I will get ill thinking of all that looms ahead. Fancy, poor me having to move!

May 21st. I feel it useless to tell Mama; it would be a fresh cause of worry. I slipped out after lunch and went to see Sylvia to pour out my troubles. I cried all the way there and back. I haven't the least notion of what to do, unless the Ferri's decide to move, then I could move upstairs; otherwise a miracle must happen. I have just seen Mrs Ferri and I am afraid there is no question of their leaving – they will pay what they are asked. The Emperor of Austria is here with his wife; I tried to see him twice, but failed –*Tant pis!* [so what!].

24th May. The miracle has happened! Mr Ferri told me that with a new law concerning property rights, landlords have not the right to turn out tenants before the end of the war. "Yes!" I said, "but he is an Ottoman and I am a belligerent" To that he had no reply, so I decided to go to the British Consulate, or rather, what stands in lieu of it, consisting of an ex dragoman, an Armenian and young Marintch [?]. I took my contract and went! Mr. Marintch was very nice, and said that my landlord had no right to turn me out, no matter what he was and what I was, and that I was simply to tell him so. "But what if he goes to law about it?" I objected. "That is exactly what he cannot do" he replied. I was really overcome by these assurances so that I could hardly thank him enough, and on leaving tried to shield my face, but he saw it [i.e.

her tears], poor fellow and he seemed touched himself.

After this I thought of making doubly sure, and made up my mind to see Mr Apikian [?]. He corroborated what I had been told. I did not tell him that I had already sought advice; he added that I must tell my landlord that my lawyer had advised me and would back me. God is really so good to me.

Last evening on my way back from Mr Apikian's, I came across two friends, both very perplexed about the chance of going away. Both know what they have [here] however bad it is, and are afraid of the unknown. Some people say the trip will be worse than a convict convoy, others that it will be as well conducted as Cook's – anyway, no-one will leave before July. Some say the English will go be sea, others by land.

1st June. Our wedding day – 31 years ago. We have brought up three children who so far have not given us a day's anxiety. Thank God, none of them have vices, and are dutiful, what more can one want?

The news are [sic] bad. Soissons is taken. God keep them from crossing the Marne. They repulsed them once; it is hoped they will do so again. I went to St Esprit on my way to the bank this morning and said a prayer for Alfred and myself. Last year I did the same, for we were married and Henry was christened there.

June 2nd. Neuilly [?] is taken – how dreadful! [The Germans had captured Reims on 29th June]. What has happened to our people? The piano has come back, as the lady is leaving. I will try to hire it out again.

Dr B left at 5am for [illegible] on the Black Sea. They have a small railroad to carry coal which is also used now for excursions; they sit on the empty trucks to go, and on the coal on their return, but it seems it is well worth it as the scenery is lovely. It rained and as he had no coat or cover he got drenched.

Two days ago there was an awful fire in the old part of the city; the biggest in the annals of Constantinople. It happened on the anniversary of the taking of the city [in 1453,] and a monster procession was to start from Fatih [an area in the old quarter,] but of course it did not take place. They say that 30,000 people are without shelter. Poor things, how will they make a home again when there are no items to be had unless one pays their weight in gold? Most of the houses were wooden, and owned by poor people, mostly Turks; there was an awful wind blowing that day and the fire raged in five different places for about 36 hours.

Subscriptions have opened; of course all the public institutions have had to subscribe. The IOB [Imperial Ottoman Bank] gave Lts.15,000. Strange to say however, anyway, it has struck me as strange, that no individual Germans have put their names down – they ought to have been the first. The fact is that no German money is ever seen about.

The news are [sic] not much better. It would be a sore disappointment to our enemies if they did not reach the French capital; they were quite sanguine at the beginning of this second offensive.

26th. I have a new lesson at Lts. 2.½ a month. I might have had 3, but only asked for the lesser sum. Sylvia gets 4. I went to the Dutch Legation, and wrote to Alfred again, so there are now three messages on the way to him; one through Spain, one through the Vatican and one through Holland. All month there have been fires; it makes one quite anxious.

July 4th. I have sold Alfred's old lounge suit which he bought 14 years ago and which he wore to do all family work in, for Lts.5. I sold it to Nina, otherwise I might have had more.

July 5th. I had a message from Tizza, sent on 13th May. She says he has often written – how is it I do not get her messages?

July 7th. This morning we had our first aerial visit. There was an awful noise of guns – everyone rushed to their windows, but all we could see was three airships, but so high up that one could not follow their movements. No one has been since, so I do not know who was who, and the result. The people downstairs were very frightened – we were not. Our men well out.

11th July. I had a letter from Nina, saying a gentleman wanted English lessons, and advising me to go direct instead of writing, giving me his address, however, he was not in, so I had to write anyway, but with no result so far.

There was such a storm. Our road has become a river; in Galata [the harbour area,] people had to remove their shoes and stockings to paddle across the road. Our airships did not do much harm, luckily or unluckily? The papers with the exception of one, ignored the noise and the event, so maybe more harm was done than was known.

It is extraordinary how thin everybody is, even people who stint themselves neither of the necessary, nor the superfluous. I cannot make it out. That we poor people who can only spend little on food, should lose our fat, seems natural, but those, and there are many, who spend from five to ten pounds a day, should get sleek, seems unnatural.

Nina [?] had not been near us for nearly three months on account of a letter; she was under supervision, in fact, she had to put up a minor detective for over a month.

16th July. Dr Bernhardt has the Spanish fever, and has remained in bed. I hope he will not give it to us. They say it is not dangerous, but still, not having a strong head, fever is always treacherous. He had any amount of his people (sanitary department) down with it. I went to see how he was and gave him the thermometer, the fly-switch and the smelling salts. I shall go to the British Relief presently – later; I did not get paid as I went on the wrong day again it seems.

23rd July. In France they are fighting mercilessly. Our Germans say that after the French and their friends have had their fling, they will have theirs. I hope they will be knocked out by that time.

Dr Bernhardt is all right again. He ate Lts.1 worth of cakes yesterday at Tokatlians [a smart hotel with a pastry shop.] Mr Flamman ate so many plums, that he is at home today – serve him right.

26th. I was called to the D.L. I supposed my message to be from Alfred. It was so, and was dated 13th May in answer to mine of 29th January. Tizza's dated 31st May reached me ever so long ago.

One would think that Alfred had made out a form which he sends each time as there is hardly any difference between one message and the other. Of course it is splendid to know that they are all well, but surely he might say something special about each one.

The French are delighted as the papers mentions their leaving. The English will have to wait. It will be a headache for me when they will have left.

On Monday we had our second raid. Six of them. There were some casualties occasioned by shrapnel. A German vice-consul was killed in front of his consulate, and a few unknowns. I was at home when the firing began, but should I be outside, I shall be careful to put myself under shelter. So far, people had rushed out to see what was happening, but I think they will keep indoors in future.

Mr Flamman left at 5 this morning (it being Friday) for the Black Sea, so that I can come into his room and write at Tizza's desk; it is nice and fresh in the afternoons.

27th. We had a night alert last night. I got up on account of Mama. It seemed pretty sharp for there was a great deal of noise. We have no details as the papers do not mention such events, but I suppose that the truth will leak out in driblets.

Meanwhile I feel sick having just paid a 342 pts fine to the electric co. I vow never to be nice to people again! Knowing that Mr Flamman likes reading in bed, I offered him a 50 candle glass [presumably a 50-watt bulb] – the one I had in the dining-room, instead of his 25, but warned him to be careful we were not caught as there would be a fine to pay. He took it out for a few mornings, but as luck would have it, one day we were inspected, and this is the result! I am furious, principally with myself, for being such an idiot as to want to oblige him. I suppose he will pay the half, but still I can ill-afford to pay this 170 pts, plus the unpleasantness of having to tell him about it.

Another unpleasant thing, Dr Bernhardt called me and said the servant had been helping herself to his sugar. He is certain for he counted the pieces. I quite believe it though she is not a thief, but I feel very shame-faced to have to accept his accusation. We counted the pieces together, and I am waiting for him to count them again when he comes home this evening. He says that about 4 to 6 pieces are missing every day. I stole two pieces more than two months ago, but dare not tell him about that for fear he should think that if I had taken two pieces, I might go on helping myself every day. I shall offer to pay for the sugar, but must catch her before accusing her, for she may deny it. He says that his honey has also disappeared. I really believe she would not steal anything else, but will he believe me?

28th. We counted the pieces together, but none were missing. He took his knife and cut 30 small pieces [presumably from a sugar loaf.] She heard the noise and asked me what he was breaking up, not being good at lying, I said he needed sugar and broke some up. I am afraid that that warned her, so she is abstaining now, but I ought to let her feel I know of it.

Another war trouble is the intermittent supply of water. Nearly every week it is cut-off for 36 hours. Luckily there is a cistern in the house. Next month I shall, or rather will, have to warn the lodgers, that my rent being raised, I will have to raise theirs, but will I have the courage to do so?

August 10th. I do not know if I must rejoice; Edythe [Tizza] is engaged to young Stack. I had a presentiment of it when she first mentioned his name three years ago. He is younger than her. Of course they have no means. His mother and sister do not look very refined (in a snapshot), I suppose however, that he is a gentleman. The fact of his mother being so nice to Tizza is a guarantee that they like her, which is an asset. How they will get on materially is another question. Alfred's announcement was very laconic and I fear he does not approve. I must say that I am a bit disappointed, but thank God, if she is happy, we must hope for the best. How dreadful to have no details.

August 11th. I have just read up all the letters I have received during the last four years. Tizza says Mrs Stack is most kind – "Irish and homely". Alfred talking of her says she "could not do more for them". As to young Stack he says, "he is only 18 [in 1915,] and a despatch rider" Freddie and Henry praise the comfort and liberality of their living, so that in that case, I suppose Mrs Stack must be the best-hearted woman in the world. Tizza adds "she is twice as fat as Mrs Chaval [?]", but what is he, my dear girl's future husband? Will he be able to keep a wife? What can a boy of Freddie's age do? How absurd if Freddie wanted to marry? I suppose that he fell in love with her and it ended by making her love him. She talks of him in her letter of April 8th, 1916, saying that he is at the front. I feel very sad to think that she will not have a house of her own, but will have to live with her husband at his mother's. I suppose that he is very nice otherwise Tizza would not care for him. Anyway, I will now include him in my prayers. God bless the boy if he loves Tizza. I don't even know his Christian name.

August 12th. Dr Bernhardt [?] has asked me to speak French to him. I replied that if in a good temper I would, otherwise I wouldn't as I had not always the patience required. It is smooth-sailing more or less in German, whereas in French we are always having to stop for me to correct him – he says *'jambon'* for leg!

August 13th. My heart is heavy and am very much perplexed. How different it would be if I could write letters to them. How to tell Alfred to accept the inevitable with good grace and not make the poor girl unhappy (if, as I think, he disapproves), by finding fault with her choice. I must see about sending my message off, for they will be longing to hear how I have taken the news.

August 16th. I went to the Dutch Legation and wrote to both Alfred and Tizza. I forgot to say in Alfred's letter that I had also written to Tizza. When will real thought-reading be invented?

August 18th. I feel very miserable. The French are leaving soon, and the English will follow I suppose. I have had enough of my life here and would go willingly notwithstanding the difficulties of the voyage. The French will go to Dedeagatch [?] and be met by a French ship which will take them to Marseille I suppose.

It looks like being a glorious Autumn day, and our two lodgers will be going out driving in Dr. Bernhardt's military trap.

August 22nd. We had another visitation last night which lasted quite a long time. [Presumably a bombing raid.] I do not know the result. Were it not for Mama, I would not get up, but though not actually frightened, the noise upsets her. The papers say nothing. How absurd! I am wondering what my new [rent] contract will contain. I expect a 50% increase, but hear that because I let rooms, I may have to pay extra. If he asks me to do so, I will have to apply to Mr. Apikian again.

August 23rd. The poor French and English are in an awful state, as they do not know what to expect. Some have sold their furniture, others have let their flats so that some are now homeless and others without furniture and dwellings. I think our people will have even more difficulty than the French. I am lucky that Alfred has not called for me, for if he did, I would have to tell him that I could not go.

August 24th. Acquaintances having heard of Tizza's engagement have come to congratulate me. I am happy that she has someone to care for her. My strongest objection is the difference in age. There ought to be at least eight years difference. I see that myself. When Alfred returns, he will find me an old woman, whereas I hope he is still a young man. With us there are only a few months' difference. Alfred however, may have made a mistake when he said in 1916 that young Stack was only 18. He may look younger than his age, for I suppose that he is fair; his mother and sister are in the photo I have. [Thomas 'Ting' Stack was born in April 1896, and she in August 1893 so he was 2½ years younger than her].

27th August. Dr Bernhardt asked me if he might have his servant orderly to sleep here and look after his clothes as he had had moth damage on two of his coats. I told him I had a room but would give him an answer in a couple of days. How I miss dear Alfred to consult with for good advice. It is no good going to Granny for she would exaggerate either for or against the question. I do not want his orderly, he would pay very little and would give nothing to Catrina. I think I will risk letting him go and find another lodger from whom I would ask 8 pounds. However, I may not get another lodger straight away and perhaps Dr B will not want to go.

Two nights ago we had a fourth aerial visit. One of Dr Bernhardt's men was in bed in his lodgings and got up to watch, when a shell fell through the roof and landed in the place which he had just left – it did not explode – what a miracle. Some people go down to the lower floors [when the attacks start]. I would not think of doing that with Mama. Luckily I am not frightened.

On Sunday, Nina & Gilbert [neighbours] went up the Bosphorus to Sariyer [the last village on the European side] by ferry with some friends. I don't know what time they left but started back at 6. The crowd already was immense; they then crossed over to the Asiatic side and back again. At each station more human freight was added till the ship seemed hardly to move. All at once, in mid-stream, the lights went out [presumably on shore], and there was a regular panic, women crying and children screaming etc. They eventually got to the bridge [Galata Bridge ferry terminus] at 12¼ and groped their way as best they could up to Pera, as the want of electricity meant no trams. They hailed a carriage (there are very few now) which asked Lts.4 to take them, so there was nothing to do but drag home the two children of their party as fast as they could. On the way, the aerial attack started again, and Nina said that they were in such a state of funk that her knees gave way beneath her.

Being out after 10 [presumably meaning there was a 10pm curfew,] both families being belligerents were afraid of the police which nevertheless went up to them twice telling them to hurry home as there was danger from the firing. They eventually got home at 1¼. Thank God I was not of the party – in these troubled times it is best to stop at home.

28th. Last night they came again! At 9pm the lights went out, and we were hoping that the worst would be over before we went to bed; half an hour later the lights came on, and we could go to sleep, but at 11½ the firing began again; it was awful this time and seemed to be directed our way. I suppose Alfred and the children will read about these raids and will worry for our safety just as I did when I heard that they had had nightly visits.

Last evening Mr Bernhardt called me to show me some figs he

had bought. He did not know how to eat them – what was to be eaten and what was not. A great many Germans are leaving for Persia to fight the English there.

August 30th. A pleasant prospect! The Turkish papers are all anxious to get rid of 10,027 belligerents. 3855 men and 6172 women – 1996 English (mostly Maltese), 3736 Italians, 1308 French and 90 Belgians. They suggest we should all be put into concentration camps and that our dwellings should be given to the victims of the late fires. The suggestion was made several times, but now, on account of the aeroplanes it seems to arise again. Fancy having to move with Granny! I do not dread the hardships of the concentration camp, for now at the eleventh hour, it would not be long before we were freed – we shall see what we shall see!

September 1st. About three weeks ago I wrote to Mr Appel asking him if he knew of anyone wanting English lessons, but he did not reply, yet he sent me a young Austrian who brought a card from Mr Appel introducing himself, and saying he would consider it a favour if I could give him lessons! He is to come four times a week and pays 3½ a month. He seems very nice and speaks English quite correctly, but not fluently. I am delighted.

I told Dr B I could not have his servant. "Why?" he said, "You have the room". I understand that he wants to have his servant with him, but now that I have this Austrian boy for lessons, I might be able to get him into this room for Lts.8.

2nd September. Now, I am bent on making money, and be able to pay Mr Grancheroff [?] back, so I have got a lot of things together to sell. It seems that calico prints etc, however old, fetch good prices.

7th September. I have begun my lessons with my Austrian pupil. He is a nice chap. We are reading 'From log cabin to White House'.

September 12th. People again speak of peace. Talaat Pasha [The Turkish Minister of the Interior], says we will have it before the winter. Us would-be travellers have to remain where we are for another three months.

Sept. 16th. There is another offer of peace, on the part of Austria this time. Will our friends avail themselves of it? Is the time right? How I want this wretched war to end, but I want us to have a peace to rejoice over, not to feel ashamed of.

Sept. 19th. The Austrian note means nothing – it is mere bluff. I see that the Bulgarians are being visited by the Greeks who are helped by the French.

I shall go to the bank to see the lawyer there so as to get some advice about my landlord's demand. I am afraid he will go over and above the 50% and ask for more on account of my lodgers. I also want to raise the rent of the two rooms, but have not the courage and put it off from day to day. There are no rooms for Lts.6 now. Why should I let them have them so cheap?

Sept. 23rd. My head is like a sieve (not a good simile). Tizza has got married! My landlord wants 14½ pounds a month plus the third room upstairs. I have lost a big sheet and poor Mama is failing mentally.

The news of Tizza's marriage was a shock to me. I have been deprived of a great joy by having this one important event of her life carried out as if I were of no consequence. I do not blame the dear girl – circumstances were against me. Why should she have waited? It would have been selfishness on my part. I suppose and hope that Henry [Aunt Edythe, 'Tizza's' elder brother – my father], was there to give her away as Alfred says he is in England on leave [not confirmed in my father's diaries]. She says she is 'dreadfully happy' – I rejoice with the dear girl and pray to God for her happiness. So far I have had to pray for him as 'Stack' – his name is Thomas it seems. He might have sent me a message of affection, but there, poor mother does not count – Tizza ought to have sent his love.

[There now follows several pages in which my grandmother writes of the problems she has in trying to get the rent reduced].

28th. What news! The Bulgarians it seems have given themselves up. If true, it is grand. Fancy dear Alfred being only two days distant [in Salonika]. What possibilities open. I have accepted to pay Lts.14 plus the room [?] I don't mind – let him fill his room with groceries when our friends come I will pick up our dear flag and we will all have a good fill! Hurrah!

October 5th. I have been quite ill and stayed at home for three days. The house business has quite upset me. The landlord came twice; I then had to tell my lodgers about increasing their rent – they were quite put out and said it was too much to pay Lts.8, so I had to go round to see about new lodgers. I put a mustard poultice on my chest and took aspirins two nights running.

It is true about Bulgaria. Yesterday Ferdinand abdicated and Boris is now king – they say we [? Turkey] will follow as the Kaiser's wings have been shorn. Dr Bernhardt told me to expect Alfred for Xmas! Anyway, this time it really looks like peace. I got out our dear Union Jack, had a long look at it and put it away at the very top of my trunk. I shall sell our Turkish flag.

How will our family organise our lives? I suppose that Tizza will not return; what will Alfred do? He is still young enough to resume his place at the bank. Henry, I hope, will not return to the OB [he too worked for the Ottoman Bank before the war], but will remain in the army. Freddie might return to the Standard Oil Company [later ESSO.] My Austrian pupil has not put in an appearance for a fortnight; I will have to run after him, for if he is still here, he must pay me for the whole month.

I hear that a young fellow who encouraged some ladies to speculate, and as the funds went down, or up, I do not know which, committed suicide. The gold pound which was up to 525 pts is now down to nearly 300.

Oct. 7th. Germany, Austria and Turkey have sent a combined note saying they accept Wilson's [Woodrow Wilson, president of the USA], 14 propositions. I am not however, confident of the result. These four years have tried me; Alfred will find that I have no go in me; I feel very limp and indifferent to everything. The lodgers have decided to stay, but will pay the increased rent only from November.

Oct. 11th. The three Allies proposition to Wilson accepting his 14 articles for peace, given last year [?], was sent a few days ago. Some kind of answer has been received, but not such a one to settle the question. I believe the Turks are ready to go to any length to have peace. Enver [Enver Pasha – The Minister of War] is doomed, and serve him right, his friendship for Germany had brought him or rather his country, nothing, and most Turks see it now. It would be in our interest that they should be made to subscribe to any terms; the same as Bulgaria.

It is lucky for the Germans that they are masters of the Black Sea, otherwise they would be in a pretty pickle. Travellers and mail will now go through Constanza [in Bulgaria.] 174 English and French left yesterday; they were advised Tuesday at 6pm that a boat would take them to Panderma, [modern Bandirma on the Asiatic side of the Sea of Mamara] at 12 am. the next day. Some were not able to settle their affairs at such short notice, and did not go. From there they would take the train to Smyrna [Izmir on the Mediterranean,] and be shipped to France. I do not envy them; I suppose that we are well on the way to peace.

Oct. 19th. The German's acceptance of Wilson's terms has not been accepted by the Entente [?]; all the Germans have been recalled from Turkey, but they cannot leave with the Black Sea being full of submarines [?]. The Kaiser is going to abdicate; Enver is getting up a revolution; the Entente is at our door; the Turks will ask for peace on any terms.

Last night Mr Flamman told me that Wilson had refused Germany's offer of peace; he was very excited, then Dr Bernhardt was also frightfully put out, and suggested that as they still had Belgium in their hands, they would wreak their vengeance on that country to bring their friends [presumably the Allies] to their rescue. It would then be war to the knife [?] and so on. I daresay that Germany will have to make further concessions sooner than going on with a losing game. Mr F said that they had one and a half million men in Russia, and a good many here. They would retrench themselves, feeling that they had friends on their oriental boundary (Prussia), and narrow their front on the West, and then they could oppose the world! They thought that Austria would not stick to them. Of course this was just Mr F's and his party's feeling;

it does not mean that all Germans think alike. It would be a joke to see the Kaiser sink! It is not charitable, but I should enjoy it.

18th Oct. God be praised, Hurrah! We are going to have peace; Peace, Peace – God be praised. It was in the papers today. It may be official this evening or tomorrow. Poor Germans, it will be so humiliating for them. I shall go out and get some figs to make jam for Alfred.

21st. Peace seems imminent yet far! The separate negotiations must not have been favourable to the nations and are therefore not given out; meanwhile there is a regular campaign against the German Alliance in the papers. It is quite astonishing how far they go. Enver kept them (the papers) in check, for the press has supposed to be free for quite twelve months. Two days ago we had two aeroplanes, one threw [?] some manifestos, and the other a bomb which made many victims – it seemed funny that whilst peace negotiations were going on, they should act so cruelly, but now the story is that it was not an aerial bomb, but a local one! Others say that it was only thrown after being provoked by machine-gun fire.

Oct. 23rd. We are nearing the end I think. Last night an English officer was seen in a Pera [main European area] street, and in the evening at the Tokatlians [one of the main hotels]. He had a big crowd around him. It is extraordinary how much more the population lean towards the English. I am certain there will be great rejoicing to see them apart from the peace question. What a change will come into our lives. What a nightmare these four years have been! My Germans don't know what is going to happen to them. A great many have left. A lot of our Austrian neighbours left this morning. How welcome will be the exchanges. If Alfred does not come straight away, or one of the boys, I shall try to let Tizza's room to an Englishman.

24th. There is a lull in our hopes again. Negotiations are dragging on it seems. The [her?] Germans hope for a general peace. They say they may have to leave at any moment – they are afraid of being kept here against their will later on. My Austrian pupil behaved most handsomely; he only took seven lessons and sent me Lts. 7½. I never expected so much and feel inclined to return at least one lira, but then thought that just now one must not 'indulge' in such luxury of feeling, so I thanked God and kept the money. I feel sorry for the young fellow, for I do not think he is rich.

25th. How dreadful to be in grief with such gladness in prospect. Some neighbours whose two sons are in the French army, have just lost their son. This dreadful Spanish fever is making many victims, particularly amongst young people. He did not go [?to war] with his brothers as he was delicate, but since he had picked up and they were pleased.

It seems tomorrow an armistice will be signed, and our dear ships will come in; there is great excitement everywhere. The Austrians in our street are leaving; they load one motor car after another. Just now we had the visit of eight aeroplanes, followed of course by firing of machine guns. Luckily mother does not realise the danger though I do not suppose that they came for any evil purpose. We are planning how to arrange the house and what to give Alfred for his first meal. I expect he will be the first to come. Mr Flamman's colleague's wives were all to leave this morning. They would leave (the Post Office), but would then forfeit their passage money from the Turks [?]. They hope the Turks will cancel their contracts. The other man says that he cannot possibly pack all his sanitary impedimenta before a week. I have an idea that he does not care to go back and then be sent to the front again.

Anyway, if the armistice implies that all Germans must leave, he will just have to go without packing. But what they are afraid of is that they may be stripped on landing [?].

30th Oct. We are no further advanced. It seems we want them to surrender the same as Bulgaria, but they hoped to have easier terms; why I do not know, so things are at a standstill. Anyway, all the German troops returned from the Dardanelles yesterday, so the Turks will get no help on that side. Our men [lodgers,] are all very excited. Dr. Bernhardt hoped to remain, but was told that all chiefs [?] had to leave, so once he has sent off all his sanitary paraphernalia; he will have to go too. The other man has just been in twice, so I suppose that something is up.

Meanwhile Austria has accepted all Wilson's demands. It was this morning's news.

I lost my pocket-book with Lts.2.3/11 [?].

1st November. Peace for us here. All Saints and all Souls be praised; the Dear Lord has given us peace. Armistice was signed yesterday; today it is official. The town is be-flagged and excited beyond bounds. The English flag excited such enthusiasm that the police told the first man (the Staces [?] I think), to put it down for fear of a disturbance. [My] ones are quite ready, but I will wait until the others officially put theirs up. All the ex-belligerents wear their colours. I told my Germans that I would put up my flag and that I hoped they would not mind – if I were in their place, I would not be so polite about it. They are given one month to go. 'Every dog has its day' Mr Flamman is anxious to go away; Dr. B just the contrary. When will I get the news which I am expecting. Surely Alfred will find a way of giving me news of himself.

2nd. I am off to the Dutch Legation (for the last time) to receive a communication from Alfred or Tizza, I don't know which. I hope it may be good news. The poor Turks are very cast down – they are disappointed. I put up my flag in the afternoon, but this morning a policeman begged us to draw it in. There were none in the Pera streets when I went to church. The man [? police] said "you put it up yesterday, that is enough". The ships are now expected, and the papers are trying to outdue [?] the general interest in the event. They laughed at the people who spent hours looking out towards Saraglio Point. [This is at the end of the Bosphorus where it meets the Sea of Marmara from which direction any allied ships would arrive from the west].

Austria has ceased hostilities with Italy, so I suppose we will soon have general peace – the Germans cannot hold out.
2pm. I went to get my message; there were two; both from Tizza saying in each that she was married, that Henry had been with them, was well and that she pitied us having to spend another

winter alone. No message again from my son-in-law; he evidently has no feelings for me. I am sorry, for I would not like to begin to being prejudiced against him. I then went to the bank and was so pleased to hear the sound of gold again! Today they were paying in gold, some of the interest of the last Turkish loan [?]. Everybody was in great joy on account of the armistice. Yesterday, being Friday [the Moslem sabbath], the bank was closed.

Nov. 8th. The ships are not through yet. Mr Flamman said there had been an accident, but I hope it is not the case. A Turkish destroyer brought four officers [presumably meaning Allied ones] ashore last night. It was all done very quietly for the Greeks are quite ready to create a disturbance against the Turks and in honour of England. I mean the Ottoman Greeks – for like our maid, they were turned out of their homes which were occupied by Turks. They have nursed their grievances till now and are very insolent towards their vanquished masters.

During the last four years we were treated as *'giaours'* [Christian infidels]. Even in public conveyances they shoved and hustled us knowing that we could not retaliate. Now the Greeks think it is their turn and do not lose an opportunity of letting them hear and feel it.

Two days ago I let our dining room to a friend, Steel, who had been shot down [?] at Adana [a large city in the south of Turkey, near the Mediterranean coast] and had been a prisoner since. He had been ill and just come out of hospital so that he looks a mere shadow. He also had no clothes apart from those the Consulate gave him, so there is not much swagger about him. He is a guest of course; he will stay until he can get away.

Dr B left on two hours notice. They were huddled like sheep and had no sleeping area. He took a fortnight's provisions with him for it will take them ever so long to get to Germany.

I wonder when I will get news of my dear ones. I am tired of waiting – people tell me I will see them soon – I don't much believe it.

Dec. 2nd. I did see my two dear sons, looking well and happy! They sent up word one Thursday at about 2½ that I was to expect them and they waited downstairs for a few minutes. I opened the door to them and was overcome with joy. They were so nice and affectionate, I did not know who to caress most and looked so nice in their uniforms. Both tried to soothe me about Tizza and spoke well of her husband. Alfred had been sent to Malta on sick leave, but would be here soon they said.

I was proud of my two sons and they seemed to get on so well together which added to my happiness. I did not see much of them as they lodged at the Pera Palace [a large hotel,] and were on duty most of the time. Henry left on Monday morning and Freddie 24 hours later. They went to Adrinople [now Edirne, the first Turkish city one comes across when travelling east from Greece or Bulgaria.] Henry was due to go to Rodosto and Freddie to Kirkklisse. [In reality the other way round.] Alfred has not turned up yet and I expect him every day as he telegraphed from Salonika on the 27th saying he would leave in a day or two, but I suppose that I must have patience for another day or two.

Meanwhile our success is taking tangible forms; the ships came through and the town is full of Entente officers and men. All the buildings occupied by the Austrians, Germans and Turks have been taken over by our people. The animation in Pera streets is indescribable; the Germans and Austrians have had to leave Pera and go over to Kadikoy [on the Asiatic side, a short ferry ride across the Sea of Marmara], ie. all those that were no able to go, for they can go as far as Odessa [in the Crimea, via the Black Sea], but the Germans being no longer friendly with Ukrania [sic], they would either have to remain there or undertake a most perilous journey to get with friendly countries [?].

Germany's armistice terms are dreadful! How happy I am not to be a German, but our victory is glorious – there will be nothing left of Deutschland, the Emperor has fled, Austria is going, or has gone to pieces; Bulgaria and Turkey have had to accept humiliating terms, but Germany's terms seem to me still more terrible. She loses Alsace, her frontiers are thrown back, her colonies are kept, and what she has to pay in the way of indemnification will be something colossal!

Yesterday the Italians took possession of the Austrian Embassy which was being built since shortly before war broke out. It is very nearly finished and now the Italian flag is flying from it. Of course, embassies are not usually occupied, but in this case it seems it formerly belonged to Italy and was taken over by the Austrians with all the belongings in it, so that they have only taken what belonged to them, but the irony is, that they [the Austrians] thought they were building for themselves, whereas it is for their enemies they got it ready.

AFTERWORD
TO MRS MARIE LYSTER'S DIARIES

The diary ends here, rather abruptly. What I find quite extraordinary is the amount of freedom my grandmother and the other 'belligerents' appear to have enjoyed; being able to live, throughout the war, with no greater discomfort than that experienced by the average Turkish family.

I have no idea as to when my great-grandmother (d'Anino/Newbolt) died; I do not suppose that she did move on to England with her daughter, and again I do not know when my grandmother herself went back to England – presumably alone – to join her husband. The fact that she was born Italian is a matter which is never mentioned in the diaries, nor which language she spoke to her mother.

No recollections or mentions of her natural father exist, so she must have been quite young when he died – see the letter unfortunately not dated – written in English to her parents, (illus. 2), which shows she attended an English school as a young girl. This suggests that her father had died when she was quite young.

I have tried to establish from the archives and website of the Ottoman Bank, now merged with the Turkish Garanti Bankasi, (www.obarchive.com) whether my grandfather did go back to work for them, and when he might have retired, but although the records are voluminous, they refer more to financial matters, and the main archive department, now in Istanbul, was not able to help. There are other pages in these three volumes of hand-written entries, in French, but nothing in Italian, but I imagine that she would have spoken to her mother in Italian. French, was then, of course, the 'diplomatic language'. How did she pick up German? The maid would, have been Greek, so she will have had knowledge of that language as well. Any knowledge of Turkish would have been rudimentary, as there would have been nil contact with Turks, as few, if any, lived in the European quarter. The references to

Catholics in the area, and the many churches she attended, even during the war, shows how wholly European this area of Pera was.

The deprivations and price inflation etc. which she refers to will have been felt by most of those living in the city. The fact that she was able to take in German lodgers despite earlier indications that this would not be permitted, either suggests incompetence by the city officials or, more likely, that they faced the fact that their European allies would prefer to lodge with fellow-Europeans, and ignored or repealed instructions forbidding these situations.

Keeping a maid might seem a needless expense, but what would the maid have done if she did not have a home? The snobbishness which comes across here and there, is probably just how any 'lady' of that class would have thought and acted.

The transcription of names has been difficult, and any person editing such a manuscript will always have the problem of consistency; for example the way she puts down dates varies. I have thus relied on the early training I received when working for various book-printers – "You follow 'copy', even when it blows out of the window!"

My father's own diaries now follow; these were written well after the actual events. He mentions his three days in Constantinople in December 1918, only briefly, and surprisingly does not mention meeting his mother.

These diaries go on right up to his time in Cyprus (1953–60) with 'Special Branch', during the emergencies there, but the extracts which follow deal only with his time in Turkey as a military man, during and just after WWI.

Notes:
* 'Harty' was an Englishman who operated a grocery near the British Embassy in the fish-market. He must have sold it, probably in the 1930s or 1940s, and it carried on trading as 'Ermis'.

He obtained work in the British Embassy – later the Consulate – being in charge of Security, and it was he who gave my father employment in 1948 when he (my father) returned to Istanbul following demobilisation. However, Harty was made redundant soon after giving my father the chance of local employment, and father was then promoted to take on his duties. This was an embarrassment to my father, but not a situation of his own making.

MAPS

Map showing Turkey in Europe, the Dardanelles, North Eastern Greece and Southern Bulgaria.

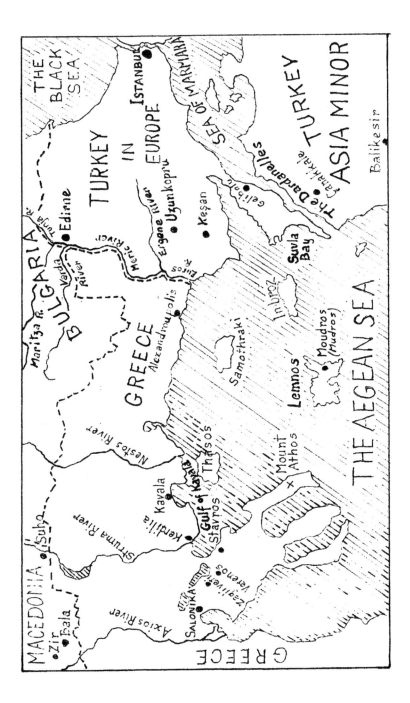

Map showing Turkey in Europe.

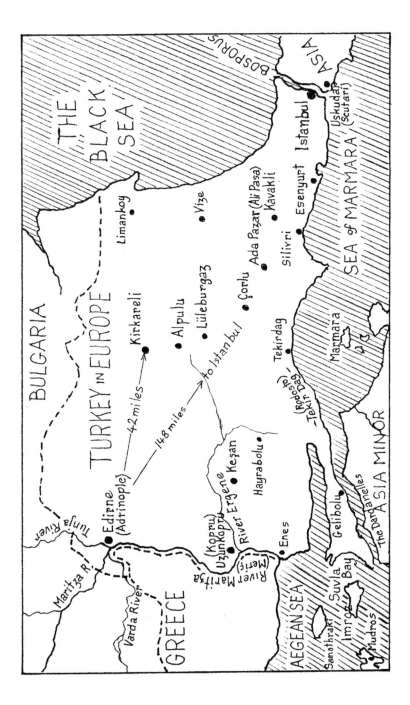

Map showing North Western Turkey (in Asia).

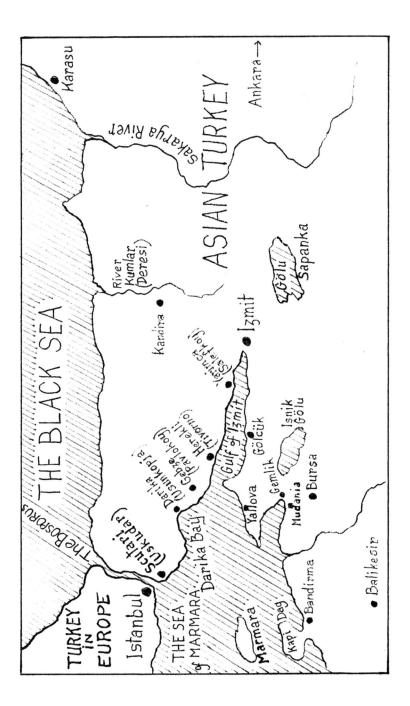

Part Two:
THE DIARIES OF
CAPTAIN HENRY NEWBOLT
LYSTER
(1888–1980)

EARLY LIFE UP TO INITIAL MILITARY TRAINING
(visits to Paris and Marseille)

I was born in Constantinople on the 6th of March 1888 in Queen Victoria's reign; of her I have only a vague recollection, but do remember going into mourning at the death of the Great Queen. My father was the Chief Cashier of the Imperial Ottoman Bank in Constantinople having been sent there by the London Head Office. He took me to England in 1903.

I also joined the Ottoman Bank in 1906, at the salary of £6 pm. which was a very good figure for a junior. I lived in Harrow-on-Hill, paying 22/6 pw. for my lodgings; my father always insisted that I should have a good lunch and gave me an allowance of an extra 2/6 for week-day lunches, without realising that I never paid that much. My favourite place was Wilkinson's Boiled Beef Shop in Coleman Street.

On returning from a holiday in Bruges in 1910, I was surprised to see the flags in Dover at half-mast, and on asking why, learned that King Edward VII had died.

I was placed in the Egyptian department of the bank, and during this time an Egyptian financial crisis occurred; telegrams kept on pouring in from all the branches, and every other day I had to spend the night there decoding the messages so that they could be answered the next day. I was paid extra for this work.

Also in 1910, the people I was lodging with in Harrow, moved to Thorpe Bay in Essex, and I decided to move with them, but then had to pay 25/- a week. Whilst in Harrow, I joined the newly-formed Harrow Rugby Club, but on moving, I transferred to the London Irish. I was also instrumental in starting the London French Rugby Club with my great friend Armand Gareau, the founder, but this did not start-up again after the war.

In 1914, there was a German, Ernest, with me in my lodgings, and on August 4th, he was with me on Southend Pier, being the only one in a large crowd who was not hoping to hear a gun being fired from Shoeburyness to indicate that we were at war with Germany, as he was engaged to a Scots girl. At exactly midnight, the gun went off, and forgetting Ernest in the excitement of the moment, we all cheered. I threw my hat into the air, the wind took it and swept it into the river – it was the first loss of the war! The crowd began to sing 'God Save the King', and then I remembered Ernest. We walked home together, and I asked him what he intended to do. He replied that he would not leave England – "How could I fight against you, my fiancee's people and all the friends I have made here?" Later on we discussed the subject again and he said "You know what a bad shot you are Henry, supposing we met facing each other – what chance would you have?" He belonged to the Southend Rifle Club, where he was a crack shot, whereas I was never very good with a rifle.

The next morning, we woke to hear that the Government had decreed that Tuesday was to be a supplementary Bank Holiday. I took advantage of this time to try to persuade Ernest to do his duty, and eventually he agreed. He packed his things, and gave me the key to his truck, his precious rifle and his bicycle, and we went together to the German Consulate in London, where we also met Alice his fiancée. We escorted him to Liverpool St. to take a train to Harwich, and before he boarded, he said to me "Henry, should we meet face to face at the front, I intend to give you the chance of firing first, but be careful not to miss me, for I will not miss you". We shook hands; Alice was crying, and the train drew away, full of Germans going back to fight us. There was no animosity, no hatred. Alice and I went to a nearby Lyons [tea-shop], and we spoke of Ernest our friend, not Ernest the *Boche*. I never heard of him again though I tried to trace him after the war. I gave his things to the British Legion to be sold or used as they saw fit.

On the Wednesday I went into the Bank to find that about half the staff were missing; some had been called-up and others had volunteered. I tried to do the same, but was refused permission and told that the work I was doing was too important, and that I would have plenty of time to volunteer after the special tasks which were to be allocated to me, were completed.

Page of diary (reduced). There are three volumes, all different sizes. This page appears in the book on pp 34.

My father, taken in Adrinople. c.1918 The endorsement clearly shows 'British Military Representative, Adrinople'.

Page of diary (reduced). There are three volumes, all different sizes. This page appears in the book on pp 34.

English School
Pera
July 15th

My dear Parents

In consequence of the great heat it has been found necessary to close school sooner than was at first intended   We shall therefore conclude our studies on Friday July 18th The Misses Walsh send their compliments

I am

My dear Parents

Your loving daughter

Mary Anino

A letter written by my grandmother dated July 15th; unfortunately no year shown. It is the style and writing of a young girl (compare the writing to the mature hand in illus.1). She signs it 'Anino', so presumably still considers herself (correctly) to be Italian despite her perfect English and attendance at an English school (that of 'The Misses Walsh')

اقامت ايتـدبكی شهر ويا قصبه	رفاقتنده بولنان زوجه واولادينك عددی	تابعیتی	اسم وشهرتی
ی ظا بوشمو هکا آبارتی نی ا ه ی نوردرکه ه بقه در	والده کی ابنو	۱ نفر	ماهام ماری بنیه انگلیش بولدک ۱۲۷۴

My grandmother's 'vesika' as mentioned on p.1. Turkey used the Arabic script until Kemal Ataturk changed it in the 1930s. The heading read 'Residence Permit for Foreigners' and is numbered 145510. Her nationality is given as 'English'. She would have been 50 in 1915.

My father, taken in Adrinople. c.1918 The endorsement clearly shows 'British Military Representative, Adrinople'.

My uncle Freddie, my father and grandfather (looking very proud of his two sons). Presumably taken in Salonika c.1916.

A photo taken of Constantinople inhabitants removing their goods from their typical wooden houses due to an approaching fire (see p.53-54). The girl on the wall on the right appears to be distressed. (IWM)   Q.14157

A group of Greek Irregular soldiers (or 'comitajis)', typical of the ones my father worked with (IWM). 8611-07

An aerial photograph showing the burning of Salonika - see p.116. (IWM) Q.90485

The following Monday, Mr Barry, the Manager called me in and I was told that I would be leaving for Paris later in the day; this gave me time to go back to my lodgings and collect a few belongings. I was given a letter for M de Cerjat – the Manager in Paris – and £100 cash and was told to put up at the Maurice Hotel there. I arrived at 10pm and booked into the hotel – the price was 50 frs, about £2 which I paid readily much to their surprise, but said they could not serve me any food as new regulations stated that no food could be served after 8pm. The next day I called at the Paris branch, and gave the letter to M Cerjat, who after reading it said that there was nothing in it which explained why I was there, so I had time to myself, and was told to report to the bank twice a day in case instructions from London arrived.

Paris in those days was a queer place. Most of the shops were closed and on the door was the usual notice that the owner had been 'mobilised'. Food was scarce and only served at certain times. Theatres, cinemas and music halls were all closed, so having nothing to do, time dragged. On the Thursday, there was a message saying that I was to meet four chaps from the bank arriving that afternoon. On going to the Gare du Nord, I found troops there dealing with refugees from the North, and found it difficult to get any information as to when the train from Calais with my four colleagues would arrive. Trains came in at frequent intervals, all of which contained refugees fleeing from the invading Germans; any organisation was non-existent. I therefore took it upon myself to put some order into this chaos.

I found a room which was staffed by American ladies from the Red Cross who were trying to issue hot drinks, and asked if I could help, and the one who seemed to be in charge willingly accepted, so I shouted to try to get people from the same village to gather together and name a mayor or someone with him to take the names. I then suggested to the Red Cross ladies that they only served those who came in with a leader who had a list of names. This took time to organise, and in the heat of activity, I forgot why I was there in the first place. It was then nearly 10pm and on checking, found that the Calais train which I wanted luckily had not come in yet. We had several warnings of when this would arrive, but it did not come in until about 4am, and I continued with my work until then. When it did arrive, there were only three of them, not four, and they were so tired that they wanted to sleep straight away.

In the morning, I advised the bank of their arrival saying I would bring them along in the afternoon as they needed sleep. M. Cerjat said that he did not see any special reason why he should meet them, preferring to deal with me. I did not see why I should stay at an expensive hotel, now that we were four, and managed to rent a small furnished flat at a reasonable price, and we all moved there, continuing with my work at the Gare du Nord, and calling at the bank twice a day.

A French colonel asked me what I thought I was doing giving orders at the station, as he was 'Commandant de la Place'. I replied that I had not seen him in the four days I had been there; we cooled down and once I had told him what I had done, he asked me to continue to help, and gave me permission to give his men orders. Several sad cases had to be dealt with, like one old lady who arrived with six umbrellas and insisted on nursing them like a child. Two women gave birth; one man kept shouting for his drink and had to be removed. It was very tiring work and I had little sleep as it was mostly at night that these refugees needed help. I then had a wire from London telling me to return, but the French colonel tried to get me to stay, but I insisted that I was only a volunteer and had to leave – he said he would propose me for the 'Legion d'honneur' for the valuable work which I had done for France! This of course never happened.

My return to London was uneventful, I went back to my lodgings for two days, then had further instructions to return to Paris. Once there, I had to go to French Ministry of Foreign Affairs to get special passes for our gang. We also contacted the railways of the P.L.M. [?] to ask for an engine to be always ready at my disposal, as our task was to save the gold bullion from the bank. The gold bars had been wrapped in brown paper, and we booked two compartments for the four of us and the gold. That was quite easy as few people were travelling North. There was no trouble until we passed Amiens, and the train stopped in the middle of a field to take on board some French soldiers retreating from a German advance. The train went back to Amiens, waited for some time and then instead of going to Calais was diverted to Le Havre Ville; it could not get to Le Havre Maritime as the bridge between the two stations had been blown-up. I left the 'parcels' with my companions, found the local station military commander and asked for his help which he readily agreed to. The porters laughed when we suggested they should get a push-cart, but when they tried to carry the 'parcels', were amazed at the weight – I told them it was lead for bullets. We were then escorted to the ship by four French soldiers with fixed bayonets, and handed the bullion to the captain for safe-keeping, retiring to the salon for a well-earned meal.

We arrived back in London on a Sunday; there were no porters and we called two taxis, sharing the load between them and started off for the City. A policeman began to blow his whistle, but I told the driver to take no notice and drive on – it seems we should have gone through the Customs House to pay the necessary duty on the bullion. We arrived at 26 Throgmorton Street and rang the bell, but it being Sunday, only a night-watchman was about. He did not know us of course, and refused to let us in. This was a strange state of affairs – we had a fortune in gold and did not know what to do with it! I paid off the taxi and we put the bars on the bank steps. I left the others and went to find a policeman, and luckily came across a sergeant to whom I explained our plight. He came with me and persuaded the watchman to let me in and ring Mr Barry who suggested I rang Mr XXX [name obviously forgotten]; this man promised to ring the watchman to tell him to let us all in with the bullion and he would come in right away. I then sent two of the others home and remained with Jones until Mr XXX arrived, who opened the safe, and once the parcels were securely placed there, we could all go home.

A few days later, we were told to return to Paris and reported back to the bank there. As there was still no firm task allocated to me, I went back to the Gare du Nord to see how things were getting on only to find that there was a new Commandant whose policy was to clear all new arrivals away from the station premises so that he would not be responsible for them. A perfect example of passing the baby.

Back at the bank, I was asked to be fitted for a waistcoat which seemed very strange, but a tailor was there who measured me and said that the garment would be ready in a few hours, and that I should return then. On returning, I put on the waistcoat and found that the garment was full of pockets, each one of which contained some jewels, the property of le Baron de Neuflize [?], and that I had to deliver the garment and its contents to Lord Oranmore and Brown [?] in London. I had a terrible journey back, what with a rough crossing and the discomfort of the waistcoat which prevented me from resting in any position. On arrival in London, I was only too glad to get rid of the cumbersome apparel, and expected at least some thanks, but nothing was forthcoming.

One night's rest, and then back to Paris. There, two of us were told to go to Marseille to try to arrange things there for an onward journey to Turkey, but although people were helpful, we discovered that nothing could be booked in advance, so returned to Paris. Whilst in Marseille, we saw the preparations for the camp that was to be set up for the Indian Divisions expected in France. Security was non-existent; everyone knew what this huge camp was for, so even the *Boche* must have known about it.

On the way back, we booked a whole compartment for just the two of us in order to be able to sleep, also buying enough food for the whole journey, but the passengers on the train began to get unruly seeing it was so crowded and we had so much room for ourselves. I spotted a French sergeant inviting him in; once he learned that we were British, he took us under his wing placing a notice on the compartment window stating that this area was strictly reserved, giving others the impression that we were spies whom he was taking to Paris to be shot. This ruse was very successful, and we shared our food with him. The journey took two days. He had been given just five francs on leaving some small outpost in Algeria, and told to report to his base near Paris. Once we neared the city we shared the last remnants of our food with the other passengers.

Our stay in Paris was now a matter of routine, calling at the bank twice a day to hear if any instructions had come. One day in September, we were told that our presence was no longer needed and we should again return to London. It seems that the idea had been to send Turkey ten million Turkish pounds as a loan to keep her sweet and on our side, but in the meantime Germany offered her two million gold pounds, and this fact, more than the arrival of the *Goeben* and *Breslau* in Turkish waters, weighed the balance on Germany's side. [Churchill, as the then Minister of War, had refused to allow two warships, being built in Britain, and paid for by the Turks, to be allowed to sail to Turkey.] Actually Turkey only got one million pounds. We were supposed to take this paper money from Paris where it had been printed, to Marseille and from there to Constantinople to be handed to the Imperial Ottoman Bank there, for signature and issue.

On our return to London, I asked permission to volunteer, and this time it was granted. I went through a stiff medical exam, and as the Sportsmen Battalion [formed by a group of like-minded sportsmen] had not been yet recognised by the War Office, we were told we would not get uniforms or pay. I was 'sworn-in' and told to return in two days' time.

I returned to the bank to close my accounts; they were very surprised at the small amounts I claimed for all my time in France. They showed their appreciation by presenting me with a cheque for £75, for which I was very pleased.

We used to meet in the bar of the Cecil Hotel, and then walk in mufti to the park [which one?,] where we were put through it by a sergeant of the Welsh Guards. Our platoon was composed of a fine set of men, some obviously over the age stipulated for admittance to HM Forces. One day we saw a company of Grenadiers march past us; at its head was a young man with a thick stick who looked as if he had overdone his route march – it was the Prince of Wales. [This would have been the future Edward VIII].

A few days later, we were told that we would be given regimental numbers, and there was competition to get the lower ones; unfortunately I was in the bar at the time, and I only managed to get 131. We then heard that a camp was being prepared for us at Romford in Essex by Lady Cunliff Owen who was the founder of the Sportsmen's Battalion. We were then told to go and get a uniform, so I asked my civil tailor to make me a smart military one ready for our march through the City. The day it was finished, I walked, full of my own importance, to Fenchurch St station, and

noticed that some soldiers saluted me. I thought this strange, but
at the station, a porter opened a first-class carriage-door for me,
and I was too ashamed to tell him that I only had a third-class
season ticket. The next morning on my return to London, a
sergeant-major also saluted me; when I asked why, he flew into a
rage on hearing that I was only a private and said he would have
me arrested for impersonating an officer. Only officers it seemed,
were allowed to have two rows of buttons on their coats. I took it
off and walked back to my tailor telling him to reduce me to the
ranks. In fact he cut the coat too short to make a tunic like those
worn by Scots regiments.

The City, hearing of our intended march, had made up their
minds to give us the bird thinking us to be a Fred Karno's unit, but
when they saw us marching like Guardees, all in perfect line with
white gloves, they changed their minds, and gave us a good cheer.

On arrival in Romford, we marched to our camp. We were 30
to a hut, 15 each side. The ablution sheds and canteen were nearby.
Privates were not normally allowed to have spirits, but we were
and had an excellent barman who prepared very good cocktails.

Many of the others in this hut were over 40; one was a Scottish
laird, named Troop, who was nearer 60 than 40, and who had his
ghillie with him acting as a sort of batman. He was a grand chap and
was able to carry on providing he drank two bottles of whisky a
day. He bought a house in Romford, where he installed his cook
from Scotland, preparing a meal for 8 of us each evening; it was
my duty to prepare a roster to detail who was to dine each evening.
On St.Andrew's Day, he gave a party for the whole unit. The meal
consisted of oysters, whisky, kippers and haggis. My job was to
open the oysters; I had 9 men with me and we worked hard at this
task for hours – I have never eaten so many before or since. The
meal was a great success although the pipes were deafening. The
officers left at about 11, and after that matters got rather out of
hand as the raw whisky was too much for some of the younger
ones. Some of us then became bearers of bodies in wheelbarrows
back to their huts.

The next party was on New Year's Eve. Ladies were invited to
this, and the expenses born by the richer ones in the unit. My
young brother [Freddie] was my guest and having missed his last

train home, had to sleep on a makeshift bed in our hut. This day also celebrated the arrival of Lady Cunliff Owen who presented us with a silver medal with her coat of arms on one side with 'God Bless You' around the rim, and on the other the arms of the Royal Fusiliers with our regimental number. [I still have this medal.]

At that time, the rumours were that the Germans were planning to land in England, and we had instructions to build a line of trenches facing the East Coast. The whole unit marched out with picks and shovels and we were to be three days under canvas. Poor Troop was wondering how he would stick it out, so we arranged that six of us would each carry a bottle of whisky for him, for his three-day ration. Unfortunately the work lasted four days, and on our way back he broke down and had to admit his real age. The War Office however, realised that they could do with men such as he, and kept him in uniform, using him for recruiting purposes.

Back in camp, life became rather monotonous; drill every day, but no rifles. Eventually bales arrived with our 'rifles', but they were only blocks of wood made to look like rifles, and these made in Japan! This nearly broke our hearts. We were all devilishly keen, us in this Sportsmen's Battalion; we drank hard, and had great fun, but we were real soldiers; there was no shirking from the parades.

One day, we heard that one of us had applied for a commission; this was against the rule we had set; we were going to go to the front as privates and as a unit. Benjamin left amidst the jeers of all of us who called him a rat. When however, news came back that he had been killed almost the day he arrived at the front, he became our hero and everyone was keen to get a commission to revenge the death of [private] Benjamin; the war might have ended before we were sent to the front as an entire unit. Everybody then applied to get a commission, and I did the same.

I was posted to the 4/3 City of London Royal Fusiliers, Territorial Battalion, and after some training was sent to Beckenham where the units were being formed. Slowly the unit grew in strength and spirit, and we started night operations; during one of these in a wooded area near Beckenham, we heard guns firing and a searchlight piercing the sky. We then saw a cigar-shaped 'thing' travelling over us – it was of course a Zeppelin; the first we had seen. I ordered my troop to disperse, as it seemed wise to do so, for we had no weapons to be able to fire at it. It went on to Woolwich where it released a few bombs. I was later accused of 'cowardice in the face of the enemy' as I had ordered my unit to disperse. It seems that we should have stood our ground and made faces at the Zeppelin as we had nothing to shoot with. It had seemed to me to be the correct thing to do. The charge was dropped later.

I was told I would be seconded to the Coldstream Guards, and moved to Windsor with my batman, and was told to go and get a proper 'Guardy' uniform; there was no room at the barracks, so I was lodged at the White Hart. We only worked three hours a day at Windsor. The first day I was placed at the end of the square, and told to give orders to a squad at the other end. I shouted at them as loud as I could, but the sergeant-major kept shouting back at me. "Can't hear you Sir!" I knew very well that he could but it was to enable my voice to carry better. My voice broke for a couple of days after this and I could drink nothing but milk, but eventually I was able to please the SM as to shouting orders. We did not get raw recruits at Windsor; they all knew their drill better than the young officers who kept being sent in to us. I was perhaps the only one who knew as much as the soldiers due to my time in Romford and Beckenham.

I was by now hoping for a posting to the Front, but the Adjutant said that as I knew my drill, I was more useful at Windsor than as 'cannon-fodder' at the Front. However, I kept asking for a move, and made myself so unpopular that they sent me back to my old unit. When, for the last time I saw the whole battalion march as a single machine with the band playing a spirited march, tears came to my eyes at having to leave this marvellous unit to return to my poor volunteers with no training.

Back in Romford, I tried to instal some of the spirit and discipline of the Guards, but it was a losing game. Good news came back of a successful engagement by our first battalion, and this brought us a better class of recruit which gave us renewed enthusiasm.

POSTING TO THE DARDANELLES
(Retreat to Salonika)

At last my orders came through. I was not going to France, but to our second battalion at the Dardanelles. This was great news. After a short leave, I boarded SS [name forgotten], and off we went to war. We were about 400 officers and 4000 men; most of the latter were Australians – discipline went overboard. These troops would not obey orders and occupied places reserved for officers, and at one time when we ran out of beer, there was nearly a mutiny. Although it was November, it was sunny all the way to Gibraltar, but the captain must have had news of a lurking German submarine, for he turned to starboard making for the Canary Isles, then turned around and went through the Straits at night at full speed for Mudros [on the Greek island of Lemnos].

Mudros harbour was full of small boats moving about. I was transferred to a small ship and put in charge of some Lancashire Fusiliers; we started off at sunset and arrived in Suvla Bay [on the north bank of the Dardanelles peninsula] at dawn. I had to stand for the whole time as the boat was so packed with men; the landing took some time as we had to walk down a plank one at a time. I mustered my little troop and was given a guide. Just as we were about to start, shells began to land all over the place. This was common, and was known as the 'morning hate'. The mules knew what to expect and were pulling at their ropes – we did not. The shells screeched over us and mostly landed in the sea; no-one seemed to be hurt. We set off following our guide and eventually came across a tent where the Adjutant of the Lancashire Fusiliers was, so I told him I had brought reinforcements. When he saw me however, he was disappointed as I was a Royal Fusilier, not from the Lancashires. I wanted to re-join my old unit, but he did not know where they were, so he rang up HQ. to ask; they sent up another guide to bring me back, but he did not know either. Later on I found my old unit which was being kept in reserve at the time. There were many men just lying about, so I asked the guide if we had been in action, but was told that they were all drunk; there were several empty bottles of spirits around – there was no mention of what we were supposed to do.

Our camp was a strange one, as the tents were all behind an earth mound either natural or man-made. Our mess was a small table placed against a rock. The latrines were a few yards from the front lines and so it was an event to use them; one had to rush to them and rush back for the Turks could see us moving and often shelled the place. No movement was allowed during the day, so that being in reserve was not pleasant.

Our turn at the front soon came, but although we were only a few yards from the Turks, things were very quiet. We went back into reserve, and then back to the front again; this time it became more dangerous as we had been ordered to save everything we could; this meant that if we spotted something by day, we had to crawl out by night to try to bring it back. It seemed an unnecessary risk, as many of the items recovered were not really valuable, but orders are orders. Whilst in reserve for the third time, we got orders to send three officers from each unit to fully acquaint themselves with the paths from the front line and the reserve billets of five different beaches on Suvla Bay. From that day we knew that the Dardanelles campaign was over and that G.H.Q. had decided to withdraw.

I was chosen to be one of the guides. The QM [quarter-master] told me that he had just one tin of Machonochie [presumably a composite meal made for the military by this maker] left, and that would be kept for this assignment. We started at dawn, and finished our maps and notes by 14:00hrs so decided to open the tin and have some lunch. We approached some Indian troops and asked them if we could use their fire, but we were badly received and learned that they had had to throw away their own food because our shadow had fallen on it and 'fouled' it. Anyway, we managed to warm up the food and started to eat – I was the loser; my two companions had spoons and managed to take a full spoon-full every time, but I just had a fork only managing to get one bean at a time. After eating, we retraced our steps checking certain points and returned to our lines by dusk.

On 23rd December 1915 we got our marching order and on the night of the 24th we left Suvla Bay, a sorry lot. Our unit consisted of only 52 men and 7 officers. All the others had gone sick; this was not surprising for although our unit had very few battle casualties, sickness was prevalent as we had no water. We were rationed to one pint a day which was heavily chlorinated and looked the colour of beer. A cold spell in November also accounted for many of the sick.

We arrived back at Mudros on Christmas Day; a nearby [military] hospital invited all the officers to go for tea, and we were very grateful to the [nursing] sisters for their hospitality. We had to help the C.O. all the way from the pier to our camp as his feet were very swollen, and he would not go sick. On our way back to the camp, I noticed a small [Greek] village, and after getting him back, I suggested that I went back and tried to buy some vegetables from the villagers [my father spoke fluent Greek]. This was agreed and I took two men with me. The village was well stocked and we bought plenty of provisions. On our way out, an officer in oilskins on a horse asked me who I was, I replied "Lt. Lyster, Royal Fusiliers, from No.1 Rest Camp". He then asked what language was I speaking to the villagers to which I replied, Greek. That seemed to be that; we were roundly cheered when the rest of the unit saw our purchases which meant we would be able to have some decent food on Boxing Day.

During the night I was awakened by an orderly who said that he had a telegram for me; this came as a shock for I feared it would be bad news about some family member. The telegram simply stated "G.O.C. [General Officer Commanding] Islands requests the pleasure of Lt. Lyster for lunch tomorrow 26th December". No signature, no indication who had sent it or who was to be my host. In the morning I showed it to my C.O. and asked him who G.O.C. was. He was not able to tell me, but said that I had to go despite my protestations that it must be a mistake and that I wanted to stay and partake of the lovely stew I had been responsible for. We asked another unit to provide transport as we did not know where G.O.C was, and I poshed myself up as best I could. On arrival, I was taken up to meet General XXX [name forgotten] who asked me "What would you have?" This was a question I had not heard in a long time and did not know what to say, so he gave me a sherry and we went for lunch; all the time I was expecting him to say that I was not the Lyster he had wanted to meet and would dismiss me. After the meal we retired to his office and he said: "Well, you don't seem to remember me, we met at the village yesterday". I had taken him to be a mounted military policeman. It was lucky that we met, he said for Salonika [presumably the main mainland British base in Greece] keep asking me to send them people who can speak the local languages, and I have found one. I protested that I did not want to go to Salonika, as I wanted to stay with my unit and go on to the Western Front with them. "I am sorry" he said, "but you will have to go as an interpreter". "Oh No Sir!" I replied, "I refuse to go as an interpreter". "You have no choice" was the answer, "as I am giving you an order". My knowledge of King's Regulations came to mind and I replied, "I can refuse Sir, as King's Regulations say that you cannot force anyone to leave a combatant unit for a non-combatant one against his wishes. I do not want to leave my unit which is in great need of manpower, and I have not as yet seen enough active service".

The General tried to persuade me to change my mind, telling me I would be more use here as an interpreter than as a platoon commander, and of the life of ease I would have at G.H.Q. This made me all the more determined to say No! Eventually he told me I was a fool and just about kicked me out. I returned back to camp, full of pride over the action I had taken and reported to the C.O. who just said 'Good Boy!' Our stew had been finished, so I only had bully beef for my dinner.

That night I had another wire [telegram]. "Lt. Lyster will report to SS *Argonaut* with all his kit." I showed this to the C.O. at breakfast, said I would attend, but would certainly return, so I only took my pack, leaving behind my valise with all my personal things. I arrived at the *Argonaut* and reported to someone who told me I was to be sent on a special mission. I tried to explain calmly that I wished to return to my unit, and how I could not be moved as an interpreter against my wishes. He flew into a temper, went out of the room and returned with the General who confirmed that I had been right in my assertion that I could not be moved from a combatant to a non-combatant unit, but said that I was to be transferred to the Intelligence Branch of General Staff, which as a combatant branch of the army, I could not refuse to join – I was caught!

WITH THE GREEK IRREGULARS
(Skirmishes with the 'Bulgars')

I was told to get my kit and go onto a small fishing boat, and that once on board I would be given an envelope with my instructions. I told them that most of my kit was still in Mudros; they promised to find it and send it on, but this did not happen. I did not even have time to inform my unit of my departure.

On the boat, I opened the envelope, which only said that I would be subject to instructions from the captain, but on asking him what I was meant to do, he only said that we would be going to places and having a look around. I was shown to a small cabin, and having nothing better to do, thought it best to get some sleep. On waking early, I noticed a small island in the distance and we landed there mid-morning where we were met by a junior officer who had a talk with the captain and then informed me that he had a suspicious character who he wanted me to watch carefully. I was introduced to my quarry, who wore a semi-military uniform and I was told he had the rank of a Greek captain, but he introduced himself as Colonel Yoannou. He spoke a strange sort of Greek, had a beard of about two weeks growth and had boots covered in mud.

The first thing he asked for, was the use of a car and this was refused, but I suggested that providing I went with him, we could see what he was up to, so the car was provided. The Greek seemed pleased that I was to accompany him, and I was told that if I did not return within 24 hours, I would be posted as missing and troops would be sent to arrest him.

What a journey; roads did not exist, and twice we took paths 'to save time', I was told, but we ended up on the edge of cliffs overlooking the sea! Eventually we did get to the village which was our destination; at first we saw no-one there, but the Greek blew a whistle, and sheepishly two or three men emerged from the houses – when they saw who had called them, they rushed forward and kissed his hands. He spoke like a leader and asked them why they were not on duty. Looking at me suspiciously, they whispered something in his ear, but he told them that I was an ally. They told him that they never expected him to come back in a car, so on seeing one, they had decided to hide in the houses to see who was coming, "for you know, we do not want people to know what we are up to". This was beginning to get interesting. A bugle was sounded and from all different angles, men started running towards us. There must have been 300, all fully armed. They fell into rank, but their eyes were more on me than on him. An 'officer' called them to attention, and then the 'colonel' began to address them telling them that they would no longer have to hide, but would be incorporated into the army under the guidance of our great allies, the British. This was received with loud cheers in which I felt like joining, and it was suggested that we had something to eat. They were obviously expecting him, as they produced a marvellous meal with the largest fish I had ever seen, and a whole lamb roasted on a spit.

During the meal, I paid great attention to what was being said around me, which helped in the compiling of the report for G.H.Q. on my return. I now knew, that rather than being a 'suspicious character', Yoannou had been building, it is true secretly, but mostly from the Royalists, an army which later became the Archipelago Division of the Greek Army, and later still the Army Corps, which he commanded.

We visited two other villages, where the same sort of thing happened, but I suggested that we should return to base, in case our people thought that he had done me in. On returning to the little harbour, I reported what I had seen. The captain was so surprised, that he suggested to the skipper that he should take us back to Salonika at once. The colonel said he would like to go too, and this was agreed, with the skipper generously saying he could have his cabin. The next morning, after having shaved and washed, the colonel looked quite a different man.

We arrived in Salonika, were met by a car and taken straight to G.H.Q. where I made a verbal report, and wanted to make a written one, but was told there was no time for that – my information would be passed on to the local Commander-in-Chief. I was to go at once to the 31st Infantry Brigade at a place called Langada, who were expecting me. I was given a car, and off we went; when we got to Piccadilly Circus [presumably a local cross-roads or similar], we asked further directions, but no one had ever heard of the place though it proved to be only a few miles further north. We arrived there and I asked for the 31st I.B., but no-one had ever heard of it, so back to Piccadilly, but again no help, so back to G.H.Q. where we discovered that the officer in charge had put down Langada instead of Langavuk! Back to Piccadilly again, but by this time it was getting dark and we were told that travelling with lights might attract enemy attention and fire. As Langavuk was apparently some 30 miles away, and it was New Year's Eve, it was suggested that we spent the night there, as they intended to have 'a bit of a do!' and in the morning they could take me to Langavuk. I found it strange that they felt that car lights might attract enemy fire, as the bonfire we lit could be seen for miles around. Drinks went round and round with everyone having to sing a song or tell a story, which became more and more obscene as the evening went on. I had been promised a call at 4 in order to catch the convoy going to Langavuk at 04:30, but no one called me, and when I woke at 6, the convoy had gone.

Being New Year's Day, I was told that nothing else would be moving east that day – how right they were. I took my pack and started to walk eastwards without stopping until 2pm when I stopped by a fountain for a drink and meal. I met no one, only seeing some small villages high up in the hills on my right. I arrived at Langavuk more dead than alive at 8, and reported to HQ. The officers were at mess so I was told to wait and eventually one Brigadier Nicholls came out shouting at me that I had been expected yesterday. I tried to explain the mix-up between Langada and Langavuk, but all I got was a ticking-off, for, as an Intelligence Officer, I should have known the difference. He then asked where the rest of my kit was, and I tried to explain that some was still in Suvla and some in Mudros, and that I had walked all the way from the transport line of the A.S.C. unit. He almost called me a liar as no one could walk all that way with a heavy pack, and he said he would seek confirmation for my story the next day.

As soon as he had left, the Brigade Major took me aside and said that I had come to a 'difficult' place, but that he would try to make things easier for me. He suggested that I slept in the mess with the proviso that I had to be up before the Brigadier woke up. The next day after ablutions, the Brigadier asked me whether I was any good at map-making, and when I told him I had never done any, it went down so badly that he said he would ask G.H.Q. for a recall. This was good news for me, but in the meantime, "you had better spent some time here road-mapping". So I was sent out to make a map of the road from the camp to Mt. Hortiak.

The only existing one was an old Austrian one of 1:10000. It started to snow and I soon lost all traces of the path which I was supposed to follow. I fell into snow-drifts several times, and walked back to camp in the evening having covered only about 3 miles; I arrived at the mess just after the officers were seated, and again had a lecture from the Brigadier, who told me I would have to miss the soup as I was late. I just replied, "Very good sir!" The next day I again tried to find the path which was supposed to lead to Hortiak, but with it still snowing it was almost impossible to find it. I therefore returned to camp and made a fictitious road report, telling the major so, who had to laugh. On the third day, even the Brigadier realised that owing to the snow I could not be expected to find a road which might have only existed in the imagination of the Austrian General Staff. I was then told to go out and make a plan of the trenches being built which were later known as the 'bird-cage'.

The snow was now melting so I was worried that I would be sent out again on the road-map quest, but worse was to come. I was shown another map and told to go to a village called Suho which was reported to be in Bulgar hands. "You will take with you 10 men, and pack mules with provisions; you will travel light; according to a map, this village is about 30 miles away. You will therefore take food for a week and will be given money to purchase food in the villages on the way, should your rations run short. Two days after your departure, we will send a despatch rider and you are to send back reports to us via him. You will all be mounted". It never occurred to him to ask if I could ride a horse – I could not!

It would have created even more ill-feeling if I had told him the truth. I told the Brigade Major that I had never even mounted a horse, and he gave instructions for a quiet beast to be given to me. I felt an awful fool trying to get on, but managed without anyone realising that this was my first time.

Orders changed several times before we set off, and eventually I left the camp with only an orderly and a Cypriot muleteer who led the mules with all rations and kit. In other words, alone I was to face the whole of any locally-based Bulgar forces. I wrote to my father what I felt would be my last letter.

We left at dawn, and set off north. By noon we had met no one and not seen any villages although the map suggested that several existed. This rest was most painful, for not being used to riding, my seat was giving me trouble despite the fact that we were going at a slow walk. By 4, we spotted what seemed to be a small village and made for it; it was dusk when we got to the first trees of this village and I spotted two men, so I approached them carefully and as they seemed to be talking in Bulgar [sic], I told my two men to have their rifles ready and I kept my hand on my revolver. Speaking in my bad Greek, I asked them the name of the village – "Suho" they replied. I then asked them which language they were speaking, "Bulgar" was the answer; "Are you Bulgars then?" "No, but we speak both Bulgarian and Greek in this village" I then asked if them if there were any Bulgars in the village; they laughed and said that if any had come, they would certainly kill them. This seemed more promising, and we rode into the village where we were royally received, with a crowd gathering around us and the traditional cup of coffee offered. I asked if there was a place where we could sleep, and the headman apologised for not being able to put us up himself, as he already had two sick British officers as his guests, but he would find room at the local inn.

I said that I would like to see these British officers, and found them to be two Intelligence Corps men with bad bouts of malaria who were delighted to see me as they had no means of communication with Salonika, and the fact that a rider would be coming out for me, meant they could get a message back to G.H.Q. The rooms at the inn were above the stables, and were clean, but there was of course, a terrible smell of dung. We had a room each and retired early, managing to get some sleep despite the constant attention of fleas and bed-bugs.

The next day I had lunch with the headman, and talked to people enabling me to write a report for my Brigadier. The two officers who had been in the village for some time could not tell me much. The next day no despatch rider came, nor the following one. He arrived on the fourth day saying he had been all over the place trying to find this village. I gave him my report and in it asked whether I was to return or to push on. He was also given a letter from the two officers for G.H.Q. The rider came back two days later, but with no further orders. I therefore busied myself with making sketches of the place and road reports. The third time he returned, he still had no further orders for me, so I wrote that unless I had specific instructions to stay, I would return in two days, but that if I was to stay, I needed more money to pay for our billeting and that of the two other officers.

No further orders arrived, and as the despatch rider did not return, we left Suho amid the friendly farewells of the whole village who came to see us off. The return trip took only 6 hours and I even managed to stay on my horse when he understood he was nearing his stables and companions and began to gallop.

I have to admit that the Brigadier complimented me on the way I had managed what he described as a 'perilous undertaking', and that my reports had been sent on to G.H.Q. I did not manage to find out how long the other two officers remained in Suho, for I never had the chance to return to this lovely village in the hills.

Our unit was then put at work digging trenches and putting barbed wire in front of our lines. Maps had to be made of these lines, and my work was to compile a daily work-map showing what had been achieved each day. It had started to snow again, and the men were beginning to complain about having to work in these conditions. One day the Brigadier went out to inspect the work of a certain unit, and found all the officers in the mess, drinking before lunch. He placed them all under arrest. As a reprisal, the men refused to work, and he had to give in. Life in this place was anything but pleasant.

One day, the Brigadier was away inspecting the front; I was left in charge when another Brigadier with other officers arrived. I explained the situation and they asked if they could see our lines which I showed them. They were not impressed with the layout, making suggestions as to how it could have been better with which opinions I agreed. They then suggested retiring to the mess for refreshments, but I had to tell them, that by order of our Brigadier, this would not be possible. There were 'No Exceptions' to the rules as to what time meals would be served! I then suggested that if they kept the following events 'Top Secret' they could adjourn to my dugout where I had hidden some drinks and some tinned food which I shared with them.

After the meal they went round the camp again, and the new Brigadier told me that his name was Crocker, officer commanding the 81st Infantry Division, and that they were due to relieve the 31st. He then said bluntly; "Are you happy here?" I replied equally bluntly, "No Sir!" to which he asked if I would like to be transferred to his brigade, and I replied that I would love it. They then left, asking me to pass on their regards to Brigadier Nicholls and he added, with a twinkle in his eye, that he regretted missing him!

Eventually the transfer took place, with the Royal Engineers appearing first to build a proper Brigade HQ. in the right places, and though my personal transfer had not come through officially, I stayed on, so when the 81st marched in, I was able to organise a housewarming party with two officers from each unit invited. What a change of atmosphere; in this mess one was met with smiles from everyone, and we became a happy family. Work was properly divided and an air of efficiency prevailed all the way through. What a fine lot they were too – Royal Scots, Argyle & Sutherland Fusiliers and the Gloucesters. My job remained to keep in contact with the villages and know my way about so that in the case of need I could guide the Brigade in any direction.

These duties gave me a fairly free hand; but in the evenings, Brigadier Crocker having learnt that I spoke French, often used to ask me to stay behind with him to enable him to practise his French and share a bottle of whisky; this often went on until the early hours, and with reveille at 7, I was getting little sleep, so he issued an order to the effect that "The Intelligence Officer, owing to his special duties, need not keep regulation hours".

Two villages in our area attracted more attention from us than others. These were Zagliveri behind us and Verenos to our left. The first-named was quite a large place with a regular market on three days a week. I got to know a local landowner, M. Agropulo, and he was able to give me information about the area. Also, as I had been made mess president I visited the local markets twice a week to purchase fresh produce.

One day in Zagliveri, I saw some French officers riding towards the market, so I waited for them. I saluted them, but they shouted at me, asking who the hell did I think I was, and what was I doing in this village. I replied that I was the Intelligence Office of the British 81st Infantry Battalion. "Where are they?" they asked and when I said about 5 miles away to the north, they laughed at me and suggested that this would be inside the Bulgar lines, and decided to take me back to their lines as a spy. I then asked them to go into the village and ask the local mayor themselves, who would explain that there was a Brigade of British troops locally, and that the Bulgar lines were some 60 miles north. This was done and through an interpreter they learnt that there were some thousand British troops in the area! This was confirmed by the timely arrival of some other British officers also coming into the village to buy provisions.

The French then took a very different line, apologising. They thought that they held the front line, and were building what they thought was the perimeter of defences around Salonika. They were the French 112st Colonial Division. I suggested that they visited our camp, and this they said they would do after reporting back to their own HQ. A few days later, I had instructions to report to the French Divisional HQ. where I would be attached for a fortnight to co-ordinate our plans. I was thus able to see the differences in the running of a French HQ. compared to the way we did things. I was given a very fine hut with a batman. Office hours were 8 to 12:30, then a sumptuous lunch after which only the duty officer of the day was on call. The first day, the general in charge asked me what I intended doing, so I said I would look around the camp and its defences. He said that that could be done later and suggested that I went with him to Salonika by car. On the way there, he told me that I would now be able to see my girl-friend there. I replied I had been to Salonika only once, and that on my way to the front. He told his driver to go to a certain house and for me to tell the lady of that house that he had sent me. "You will be made at home there, and a nice selection of girls will be brought out for your delectation", he said, "but do not pay more than 25 drachmas". He would call for me at 7pm.

I did not avail myself of his offer, but had a look around the town stopping at a famous pastry shop, 'Floca's', and went back to the *madame's* house for 7pm. where he picked me up and was incredulous that I had not taken advantage of the situation I found myself in.

My opposite number in the French camp was *Chef du 2me Bureau*, and as such had a large staff of photographers, map makers and statistic holders under him, with maps and diagrams everywhere. Despite all this, they did not know where the front lines were, nor that we British were miles ahead of them. I altered their maps, traced out our proposed work, made a rough tracing of the road to Suho giving them as much information as I could. My stay there was a nice change, and thought I did not learn much, it was a very interesting experience. I returned to 81st I.B. with a good supply of French delicacies; this made my return even more welcome.

Life fell into a routine; one day however I decided to visit the Royal Scots, on our right, who were the only unit I had not visited. It was a hot day and when I got to their lines, I met an officer in shorts and short-sleeved shirt who told me that I would need to speak to their CO., one Col. Callender, but when I got to see this man, I had stupidly forgotten his name, and called him Col. Almanac. He was furious and placed me under arrest, made me take my belt off and sent me back to my unit where I had to report to our brigadier. I did not know whether to laugh or cry, but luckily the brigadier did not see it as a serious matter, although I had to remain confined to barracks for 48 hrs as a token punishment for my disrespect to a senior officer.

Due to a change in the political situation, we were asked to move east towards a small place called Stavros in the Gulf of Cavalla. I was made the guide although I had never been that way before. I had to move forward with the advance party, find a suitable place to camp and then return to the main unit and guide them by night to the chosen spot. This routine continued for three days with the result that I had no sleep for this time. At one time I almost fell off my horse due to tiredness, and took a strong tot to keep me awake[?]. On my final return, the brigadier accused me of being drunk on duty, but I explained the situation and he allowed me to sleep in his own tent and told me not to resume duties until I was fully rested.

The R.A.M.C. [Medical Corps] did not approve of most of the sites which I had found; too many flies, – no clean water etc, but I had to choose sites which I felt were safer from discovery by the enemy.

We had not been in Stavros for long, when order came from HQ for someone to go on to Cavalla, and being the only Intelligence Officer in the unit, I was told to go there. Not knowing the situation there, I suggested that I should go in civvies [civilian clothes], but this was over-ruled. A small trawler was put at my disposal. My arrival in Cavalla caused something of a stir, and was asked [presumably by the Greek authorities] if I had any papers. I replied that I was only wanting to call on the British Consul in the port, so I was accompanied to his office, but was very badly received by the man, who accused me of compromising his position by calling on him. I pointed out that he had the Royal Arms on the door, over the words 'British Consulate', so could not see how my presence would make any difference, and that I had been sent on from G.H.Q. to find out the position in the area. To my astonishment, he said he had none to give me. I then asked if he could put me up for the night, but he refused to do so, and suggested that I stayed at the Hotel Khedivial, asking me not to return to his office again.

At the hotel, I was given a room by a lady; by her accent, I presumed that she was German. It was still fairly early, so I went for a walk around the town and stopped at a café and ordered a beer, pretending not to notice the attraction I was causing. A civilian approached me and asked if he could join me; I said I would be delighted; he whispered that I should leave this cafe discreetly and go to another place where a Greek officer would meet me and give me some information. I found the other café, and was shown to a table at the back; I would not normally have accepted one so far from the door, but presumed that this was necessary at this particular time. A door opened behind me, and Greek captain beckoned me inside. He said that he was a Venezelist, but that most of the [local] artillery officers were Royalists, with the result that their guns were gradually being dismantled and being sent to the Bulgars, so that when they attack us, we will have no artillery to defend the town. If you go to the gun positions, you will be able to see for yourself that they are nearly empty. He suggested that I should go there the next day, after he had tipped off the sentry on duty that I would be visiting, for it was a prohibited area.

I thanked him, telling him I would do so and told him I was staying at the Khedevial. He said that it was not only the HQ. of the Royalist clique, but also that the two German ladies there ran the German spy system locally. This was not pleasant news, and on returning to my room later, found that the door did not lock. I placed a chair against the door, and slept fully-clothed with my revolver close by. The following morning I went to the place which had been suggested, and as I had been told, saw two empty gun positions. I was challenged by a sentry, who luckily was the one who had been tipped-off by yesterday's Greek captain, I made some drawings which he chose to ignore, and moved on quickly as he confirmed that most of his officers were Royalists.

Back to the hotel and I found myself being questioned by many people on military and political matters. I stated that I was just a lieutenant and knew very little, and that I was merely visiting Cavalla to see if it would make a good place for the officers of my unit to come when on local leave. I do not think they believed me, but I had to kill time until the boat called back for me in the early evening. I was very happy to get away, and felt that the information I had gleaned was useful; I filled in a report and expected it to be sent to G.H.Q. This did happen, but they decided it was not important enough to act upon, and quite soon the Bulgars marched into Cavalla, virtually unopposed, with very few Loyalist Greek soldiers being able to get away before being captured by their arch-enemies, the Bulgars.

Our mission at Stavros [having] failed, we were told to return to our former positions. Our job was now to send parties along the shore towards Cavalla to check whether the Bulgars were advancing towards our positions. The political situation in Salonika had worsened. A certain Greek leader nicknamed 'Panda Fegho', had taken to the hills with about 2,000 deserters. These began to attack our convoys and we were given orders to try to stop them. These hills had no roads, and the horses had to follow in single-file making it easy for the brigands to pick us off one by one if they had so wanted.

My position was now with a Yeomanry squadron, but was ambiguous as Intelligence Officer and Political Adviser. The CO. was too concerned as to what 'G.H.Q. will think', and would not move without asking authority to do so. By wasting time this way, one could not act on information received. I had become friendly with a certain monk on Mount Athos, and he had told me that all the leaders of the deserters would be at a certain place to celebrate a certain saint's day, and I suggested to the CO. that we took the whole squadron to this place and captured them all. This was considered 'too risky' of course and he sent a pigeon to Salonika to request permission for this action; we had the reply by despatch rider two days later by which time the feasting was over.

The major decided to have a look at the place anyway, but instead of going on foot through the forest, he insisted on travelling by horseback in single file, and so our movements were watched from the moment we started; when we arrived at the village we could see that there had been a great feast. This was reported to G.H.Q. who sent us orders to stop any interference to our movements, but not getting any co-operation from the major, I decided to act alone, and the following morning left the camp early, unarmed, and made for the hills. After about two hours I was halted by two sentries as I expected to be, and informed them that I wanted to talk to their leader, and pointed out that I had come unarmed. I was blindfolded and led on; when my blindfold was lifted, I saw an extraordinary sight, with well-armed troops and well-camouflaged tents all around. A man I took to be Panda Fegho came forward and asked if I spoke Greek. I answered in the affirmative and asked if I could speak to him privately. We went into his tent and the traditional coffee was brought in. He laughed telling me that the sugar came from our own convoys. I said that I was glad he had mentioned the convoys as it was those I had come to speak to him about.

"Our HQ's are getting fed-up with you" I told him. "and as long as you were just Greek deserters, we were not interested in your activities, but now you had begun to attack our convoys, we have begun to treat you as enemies, and will retaliate with force. This will mean bloodshed which would be a pity. I have come on my own initiative to suggest that you stop your activities, and I will try to persuade our side not to attack, providing each of your men returns to our lines with his rifle". I then asked him to allow me to speak to his men, and much to my surprise, he agreed, and I felt that he thought he could not keep them together for much longer. He gave some orders and his men sprang up from all-around. I told them that they could not remain in the hills all their lives and put my proposal forward. This was not well received especially as I insisted that only men who brought their rifles with them would get the full amnesty. I told them that this was only my own idea, and that I would have to get permission from our HQ. to agree.

It was then decided that we would meet in a week's time at a place to be agreed, and I would try to get G.H.Q. to confirm my offer when we would hear whether they had also accepted. I was put back on my horse, again blindfolded and taken back to the place where I had been 'captured'. I parted from my two guides on the most friendly terms.

Arriving back at the camp, I told the major what I had done. He was of course furious, but could not stop me sending a long detailed report to G.H.Q. in Salonika. Luckily their reply came back in time; they agreed. We then started to make 'birdcages' [barbed-wire enclosures used as temporary prison cages] for these men, estimated to be about 2,000, and shipping was sent for to take them back to Salonika. On the appointed day, I met their delegates and told them that they could all give themselves up with a free pardon apart from Panda Fegho himself, as the Greek command did not feel they could accept him back as he had been the leader of the desertion. It was agreed that they would march down a certain route with rifles at the slope starting at 08:00hrs.

On the actual day, we prepared food for about 2,000 men and by 10, some 600 had appeared, surrendered their arms and been put into the cages, but suddenly we heard firing coming from the direction of Mount Athos; the intensity increased and the men in the cages began to get nervous, so we had to call out all our troops. I went towards the firing and found a Marines officer who asked me who the hell I thought I was, and told his men to rush off and pursue the retreating Greeks. I tried to get him to stop and tried to explain that he was firing on and killing men who had come to give themselves up, but he would not listen. Eventually there was a lull as there were no more to fire on. It appears that he had had instructions to land somewhere between Mount Athos and Stavros and try to come to grips with a body of Greek deserters. Needless to say, no more of the deserters came down from the hills; they thought that they had walked into a trap, and that we were even going to massacre those who had willingly surrendered their rifles. Obviously there had been no co-operation between the Army and the Navy, which is the only explanation for this sad incident.

Panda Fegho hearing of this 'trap', as he understandably interpreted it, was furious, and thus for the first time we came under fire from some of his men, and this was reported to G.H.Q. as well as the details of the Navy's interference. We heard no more for a few days until we received instructions to take part in a combined attack on the rebels' camp with some French troops. They were to carry out the main attack, driving the rebels towards our lines, or at least that was the plan, but the only danger came from the French themselves who took us as the enemy and fired a few shots until they realised who we were. The rebels faded away and we entered the camp where I had been some days earlier. The French had orders to pursue the few remaining rebels to Mount Athos where they were supposed to have taken refuge, but they did not cover themselves with glory and some of the monks came to us for protection, bringing with them some of their valuables for safe-keeping.

After this episode, life resumed into a normal routine. One day I was on the shoreline watching troops disembarking when I heard my name called, and there was my young brother Freddie. He had been appointed Interpreter Officer to the 80th Infantry Regiment.

I had no idea that he had even left the UK. We only had about 30 minutes together before he had to get into a staff car to report to his own headquarters.

I used to go out nearly every day along the Gulf of Cavalla; this went on for some time until orders came for me to rejoin my own HQ. which had moved back to the Struma valley. I had to go along the Seres Road [?] which was being built by the Royal Engineers. During my absence, changes had taken place, and Brigadier Henry Crocker had been moved to the 28th division, to be replaced by Brigadier Widdrington, a K.R.R. [Kings Royal Rifles].

We were all wondering how we would get on with the new man, but soon he proved to be most popular with his concern for the well-being of all the troops under his command. We had a meeting in his private study and hearing that I was mess president told me that he wanted our mess to be the best in the area without the mess bills going up – he would make good any shortfall personally. In addition he wanted me to make a roster of all the officers and to list of four of them to dine with him at each meal. He explained that he being a Green Jacket, some of the Scots in the brigade rather resented his arrival, so was determined to make the unit a happy one.

The work was hard, as the Struma Valley was a death-trap from a health point of view due to the mosquitos and malaria; soon our units became depleted as these vile insects were everywhere. We dug ourselves in at the foot of the hills, and every now and then reports from G.H.Q. suggested that the Bulgars would attack, especially when we heard that General Mackensen [a German general!] had visited the Bulgarian lines. I was given the task of knowing the way back from the front line to the bird cage, [defensive position behind barbed-wire perimeter,] over the hills in case we were pushed back. I went alone and was away for four days living off the land.

During this time, I was on top of a mountain range in the sun, not wearing my regulation sun helmet. I noticed a company of officers in the distance and on checking with my field-glasses as to who they were, saw that they included the C.i.C. [Commander in Chief,] who was also looking at me with his own glasses. Knowing what a stickler he was for discipline and knowing that I was not wearing my sun-helmet, I got back on my mare and galloped off. Looking back I saw that they had dogs with them, but I knew the land and they did not, and to lose my scent, I crossed several small brooks, soon realising that they had lost me.

On returning to camp, I spotted a notice which stated that the officer who was at a certain co-ordinate on a certain date was to report to the Corps HQ. at once. I went to our Brigadier telling him that I was the officer to whom this referred, but he suggested that I did nothing more about it – which advice I followed faithfully.

I came across the C.i.C. [General George Milne] on another occasion, when I returned from leave in Salonika having met up with my father and brother there. I arrived at Brigade HQ. to find that all the staff had gone out for an early morning inspection of the trenches, having left a note for me to that effect. I was shaving when an orderly came to tell me that some high-ranking officers had just arrived. I went out to meet them, and to my horror saw the C.i.C., with some of his staff officers, and was luckily able to advise them that the brigadier was out on an inspection of the trenches, telling them that I was the I.O. (Intelligence Officer).

The general then said that he would go and inspect them as well, and asked for the positions of the men in the trenches. I replied that the Camerons were on the right, the Argyles in the centre and the Gloucesters on the left with the Lovat's Scouts [?] in reserve. As I said that, I realised that this had been the situation before I went on leave, and that the brigadier was probably at the front, changing their positions for that had been discussed before I went to Salonika. I was in a right pickle! Luckily one of his staff officers said that it looked like rain, and I jumped at the excuse which had been presented to me, saying that when the wind came from that direction, it usually brought rain and any consequent storm could be quite severe. The general then decided to return, telling me to tell the brigadier that he was sorry to have missed him, and off they went.

I rushed back to the office, and looking at the current map, realised that every one of the positions I had indicated to him and his staff, was wrong. I reported all this to the brigadier when he returned, and he was really angry with me – and quite right too. But the general never discovered that I had given him incorrect information, for which I was very thankful.

The 10th division was still in the Salonika area, and one of its brigades was ordered to attack the villages of Balla and Zir just over the Struma river; this was to take place on a Sunday, but we were not to take part but retire to a rise about half a mile away and observe. The attack failed with many casualties which we could observe with frustration at not being ordered to take part. The following Sunday we attacked again with the same result. A week later, it was our turn and we were told we had to hold the villages, but with the knowledge gleaned from the previous attacks, we did not advance from the east as there was a large deep pond which protected the village of Balla. The Argyles and Sutherlands did the first attack with the Royal Scots in reserve. My duty started the day before as I had to show the Royal Engineers the spot I had chosen for them to build a bridge across the Struma. They did a good job and we covered the floor with straw to muffle the noise of the guns which went over, then the infantry. The R.C. padre held a short service for those of his faith [my father was a Catholic.] It was a most impressive and moving service, for some of the men did not come back.

At dawn the artillery opened fire and we realised how much better we were served than on the previous attacks. The Argyles on the right were met with heavy machine-gun and rifle fire. This battle has been well-reported in the official report[?], so I will not repeat the details, but I will mention a particular event when a pipe major of the Royal Scots calmly walked in front of his unit when they were told to advance. He was hit several times, but continued to play his pipes. He eventually fell, and I put a cigarette in his mouth as he was carried away on a stretcher. I am glad to say that he survived his wounds. The enemy retired at last and the Engineers put up barbed wire at the front of our new positions. The next morning the Bulgars did try to take back the villages, but the wire held them back and they had heavy casualties.

On the Monday morning following two sleepless nights, I was put in charge of the prisoners; there was only one officer in the bag, a captain; he was put into a ruined church and had been offered food, but had refused. With the help of an interpreter he explained that he was not going to be bribed with good food, and would only eat what we ate. Asked what he meant by this, he explained that they knew that all our supply ships had been sunk by German submarines, and that we were starving. I assured him that he was being given the same food as our men. This he did not believe, so I took him to the kitchens and showed him the splendid food which was being prepared for all. He was then furious with his own people for having deceived him, and asked if he could be allowed to return to his side to tell them the truth about the supplies situation.

This gave me the idea of placing loaves of white bread near the Bulgar lines with a notice stating "come to us and eat this sort of bread." This was done and we obtained useful information from some deserters who took advantage of our offer.

Having fought so desperately for these villages, we had to abandon them in the summer, as the danger of malaria was greater there. We then left the right bank of the Struma and took to the hills again. Patrols kept checking, but there was no sign of the Bulgars wanting to advance back into the plain except for the line which they held at Barakli, but we took that back from them in the autumn when we crossed the Struma to set-up our winter lines.

What a winter that was! The Vardar winds [?] blew and blew. During the battle when we took Barakli, I was in charge of the brigade base HQ. In the thick of the fighting when I was on the telephone, General Crocker, now commanding the 28th Division, turned up and asked how things were getting on. I gave him the picture as I saw it – he said it was too cold and dangerous to go any further, and produced a bottle of whisky which we shared.

[My father's diaries now wander off into some time he spent at a hospital after being wounded in a night patrol and into descriptions of a great fire which engulfed Salonika in August 1917.]

I returned to my unit in the Spring, and a [British?] observation balloon had appeared on the 28th Division front. It could be seen quite clearly from our position. A rumour went round that the Bulgars had sent a message that on a Sunday, a plane would be sent to destroy it. Sure enough on the following Sunday, a *Boche* plane appeared, and fired on the balloon which went down in flames with the observer coming down slower with his parachute.

Later in the week the same thing happened. However, when a third balloon went up, this was 'booby-trapped', having been loaded with explosives and unmanned, so when the pilot neared it, the explosives were detonated from the ground, and one of the wings of the plane was separated with the main body falling to the ground with a crash. We thought this was a dirty trick and we buried the German pilot with full military honours. Photos were taken and these flown over and dropped over the Bulgar lines to show the enemy our respect for the brave pilot.

Life was now getting boring. Staff had to entertain the troops with travelling theatrical parties. 27th and 28th divisional HQ. had their own shows, and so had 738 MT. [Motor Transport] Co. who had a very good show called 'Slip Your Clutch'. Horse races and polo matches were also arranged. The brigadier, General Widdington asked me why I did not partake in the polo matches as my mare seemed like an ideal polo pony, so I replied that she had a mouth like a steel trap and did not take kindly to spurs. He laughed and asked if he could ride her the next day, to which request I agreed riding her over to the polo field and handing her to the general. He must have touched her with his spurs, for the last we saw of him for some time was a cloud of dust on the horizon. The match was nearly over when he returned. I liked my Nan and we understood one another.

In June 1918, my turn for home leave came up. I got my marching orders and travelled south from Salonika to Lamia, then westward to the coast where we took a boat to Otranto on the heel of Italy. The railway journey to London was very well organised with long stops every day for a hot meal and the locals usually provided some sort of entertainment for us. On arrival at Asti, I recognised the name and asked if I could buy some of their famous sparkling wine. I was told I could purchase a case of 50 bottles at a ridiculous price of about 6d [old pence] each. We got this back on the train with some difficulty; the CO. on board was not happy with this purchase, but when I opened a bottle and shared it with some of the chaps near me, word got about that I was selling 'champagne' at only 1/- a bottle [one shilling], he came to taste it and said he would buy all that remained from me.

I spent my leave in London, arriving on August Bank Holiday

and visiting many theatres, and even seeing 'Lilac Time' twice. On my last day I took the train back to Southampton where the R.T.O. [Rail Transport Officer], told me and several others that the Bank Holiday did not count as leave, and as such we had arrived a day early, meaning we had to spend another day either locally or returning to London. I went back to London and took my sister-in-law out to the theatre. [This would have been 'Sweetie' Stack, the sister of Thomas Neville Stack, R.A.F. who had married his sister/my aunt Edythe, known as 'Tizza' – see p.57 in my grand-mother's diaries].

The return journey was not so pleasant. I had to share a compartment with a colonel in the A.P.C. [?] as the O.C. [Officer Commanding] of the train he had been allocated a carriage, but with broken windows and we suffered from the cold as a result.

On my return to Salonika I was told to report to 27th Divisional HQ.'s and was told that they had moved to the right bank of the Varda River from the Struma Valley. I was surprised to find mostly French officers about as they had not fully handed-over operations to us. I met my opposite number from the second bureau ['Deuxième Bureau', a French counter-espionage service.] who took me to his office; this was a large hut sub-divided into many sections for storage, development and dark rooms for the photographic equipment which they had. He handed over to me literally thousands of aerial photographs and said that I needed to order our own air forces to keep up the air reconnaissance, as this was the only way we could tell what the Bulgars were up to. I could not tell him that this was not feasible as I did not have the staff capable of doing this work. Still, I learned quite a bit as to how to interpret air photographs. This officer stayed with us for a few days, and then the French left completely: we tried to do our best with the few staff and scant information at my disposal.

One day I awoke late following a long day at the front trying to see the lay of the enemy lines, and found the camp in disarray as it seemed there had been an alarm due to a rumour that the Bulgars had sent over some poison gas shells, and everyone except me had taken to the shelters, but luckily this had not been the case.

At last we had made all our preparations for the 'Big Advance'; my assignment was to be liaison officer to the Greek corps to our left, and there I found in charge my old friend [now] General Yoannou. He too was pleased to see me, as no-one else had been able to speak Greek. We worked together over details, but of course things did not go all that smoothly once the attack started, following the heaviest bombardment I had ever heard. I was at the extreme left of the attack, and once the Greeks started to advance, reported their positions to our corps, but the Bulgars seem to have retreated faster that expected and I found that I was with the Greek reserves, the front line having moved on faster than our own troops. This created a large gap between the two forces and one which could be exploited if the Bulgars noticed. My instructions came back to tell Gen. Yoannou to hold back, but his response was that if we could not march forward, his troops could and he would not stop until he reached Sofia [the Bulgarian capital.] I was then suddenly given orders to return to G.H.Q., so had to comply, so never saw the whole operation through.

Back at HQ, we were on basic rations and I was asked to go out to some of the villages to see if I could obtain some eggs. I went out and on my asking in my best [limited] Bulgarian '*yaiza ima?*,' the villagers always shook their heads. This I found frustrating as I could see chickens running around, and felt that they did not want to sell us anything. I later learned that shaking one's head in that area, meant 'Yes!' I then received further orders to return to Salonika, and on my way there suffered some sort of mental breakdown. The last I could remember of my journey south was resting under a tree and allowing my mare Nan to graze freely. I woke up in a bed in a hospital in an island just off-shore from Salonika; I had been unconscious for two days, and no-one could tell me how I had got to the island or what had happened to my mare Nan, whom I never saw again. I was kept in the hospital for about a week though felt quite well again after a couple of days. I was not allowed to contact HQ, so decided to abscond. I found out that a ferry-boat left the island twice a day, so took one of them and reported to G.H.Q. advising them that I was now again fit for work. I was told that I would be court-martialled for leaving the hospital without a proper release, but this was changed to a disciplinary board where I was given a reprimand for leaving the hospital without permission.

As chance would have it, my father was also in Salonika [as a former bank official, he was with the Royal Army Pay Corps there, though then a man of 53], and we were able to spend some time together. I learned that I had been recalled to G.H.Q. as an attack on Turkey was being planned through Adrinople/Edirne, but as the Bulgarians had capitulated, and so would Turkey, the planned attack never took place.

We then heard of the Mudros Capitulation [this was on 30 October] by which Turkey also formally capitulated. I was detailed to board a steamer which would take me to Constantinople.

[It is surprising that he does not say that his brother was with him – though it is mentioned further on; or that his mother was there, having been in the city ever since the war begun. Their meeting with her, so well-recorded in her diaries – see pp.70-71, does not warrant an entry here! The date, according to her diaries was December 2nd].

We arrived in Constantinople late in the evening, and three of us [I presume these to be my father, his brother Freddie, and the name Macray (sic) is mentioned] of us went ashore to meet the Turkish General Staff to arrange for the main landing which was to take place the following day. After having made the arrangements, we went to the Tokatlian Hotel for a drink before returning to the ship for the night. There were German officers there, and they stood up and gave us a stiff salute. We were not sure how to respond to this token of respect. We asked for cocktails, and were brought some awful mixture which we refused to drink, but the waiter apologised saying that they had had no supplies of gin or vermouth for about four years. We returned to the ship and the next morning our troops disembarked; we were told to spend the night at the Pera Palace Hotel, but on getting there, we learned that we had been given the servant's quarters as the German officers still had all the main rooms.

I had some £75 sterling [presumably sovereigns] with me and went to the Ottoman Bank asking whether it would be better to change it there and then or wait for a better rate. The manager offered me his 'preferred' rate of 108.56 piastres to the pound which I accepted, but the next day the official rate went up to over 600. I was furious.

POSTING TO ADRINOPLE/EDIRNE
Appointed as Military Governor of Eastern Thrace

I spent three days in the city and then was told to go to Saranta Eklisies [Kirklareli in Turkish.] We left Sirkeci station; four of us. Lt. Col. Samson, my brother who was to go to Rodosto, and another officer [presumably the previously-named Lt. Macray] for Uzun Keupru. Col. Samson was to go to Adrinople/Edirne, where he had been consul general before the war. I left the main party at Alpulu, a junction for my town, and arrived late at night to be met by a Mr. Cokinos who had been acting consul there before the war. I was given a wing of his house, and he found me a cook, Despina, who had been the cook for the French consul before the war.

The next morning, I called on the *Mutesarrif* or local governor of the area and asked where I could find the Turkish local army commander. His reply was rather staggering – "Through the fault of the army, we have come to this situation, so I have sent him and his family to the stables". I asked to be taken there at once and found the poor Colonel Shukru in a bad way. I told him that I would instruct the governor to find him and his family better quarters. Later I became quite friendly with this man. My position was known as Military Control Officer, and my job was to see that the local Turkish troops deposited all their arms at a certain place, and then remove some of the vital parts and keep them separate. Shukru's division was very much depleted due to desertion. I had to report to Col. Samson every now and again, and he would instruct me if anything else needed doing.

One day, on a routine visit, with my Turkish driver driving, the car left the road, overturned, and we were both pinned under it. I managed to get out, but could not release the driver. Luckily I saw some men on horseback galloping towards us; I could not be sure if they were deserters looking for some loot, but they stopped to help us and managing to lift the car, got the driver out. The poor man was hurt with a dislocated shoulder and other injuries, and was in great pain. I made a sling for him, and the men suggested we went to their village.

On arrival there, an old woman saw to my injuries – a gashed knee, which she treated with warm water in which she had infused some herbs. I asked if someone could telephone Adrinople to ask for a relief car to be sent, and to tow in the damaged vehicle, and as this would take some time, asked if we could be given some food. This was agreed, but the food seemed to take a long time in coming, so I asked why and the Head Man there told me that as this was a Muslim village, they had no wine, and had sent a man to a nearby Greek village to obtain a bottle for me – that was real Turkish hospitality. We had a lovely meal for which they would not accept payment, saying that Allah wanted them to help people in distress. On my return I sent them some gifts as a token of our appreciation for their hospitality.

On some day later, the colonel wired me to come to Adrinople with enough kit for a week-end. On arriving on a Saturday, he advised me that his eye-sight was failing, so he was going to Constantinople to have it seen to, and that he would be back on Monday, so he did not intend to give me the keys to the safe. On the Monday morning, our *cavas* [uniformed porter] advised me that a local Greek delegation, headed by the Bishop of Adrinople, with all his synod, wanted to call on me. I said to send them up to the office and they congratulated me on my promotion. I did not know what they meant, but they said that I was now Military Governor and Control Officer for Eastern Thrace. I informed them that this was wrong, and that Col. Samson, who would be returning soon, held that position. They advised me that he would not be returning. I insisted that if he was not returning, that another colonel would be sent out to replace him. By the Wednesday, he had not returned and so I contacted HQ in Constantinople, who confirmed to me that the colonel was on his way back to England. The next day I had a letter from them with the key to the safe telling me to take over and that another officer would be sent to Kirklareli in my stead. This eventually happened with the post going to a Captain Sandford, a regular who proved to be a very nice man.

There was little of much help in the safe apart from the reports from the three areas under Adrinople control, so I asked the colonel's secretary what the work consisted of. He said that Col. Samson had been very secretive, and that I might learn more from a certain Mr Funduklian, in the city. I made contact with this man who owned a local flour mill, and who had made a lot of money from the war. He told me that Col. Samson paid him £20 a month which he gave out to his local contacts for information. He was reluctant to tell me who these were, but I insisted, and he gave in, but the information proved to be of little value so I started to nose around, and established my own independent sources.

One day, an inspector [?military] turned up, and asked to see my accounts. He found that I had over £600 in the local branch of the Ottoman Bank, and asked why I was not using it. Apparently Col. Samson was getting £200 a month, and used it, so why was I not doing the same? This made me wonder if my reports were not good enough and asked whether this was the case, but they replied that my reports were excellent, so I suggested that they did not send any more money until I asked for it.

Our staff in Adrinople consisted of a Lt. as a secretary, a signals officer and 11 other ranks. I also had under my command for technical reasons, an Italian battalion – the 1st bn. of the 62nd regiment. The only officer there who knew any other language, was a Capt. Gonzi of their machine-gun section, who spoke French. I had several meals with him in their mess and tried to pick up their language, becoming fairly proficient in it by the time they left, two years later.

A few weeks later, the local governor called on me and informed me that large-scale contraband was being smuggled into the area over the Bulgarian borders by some Italian soldiers. I accused him of insulting the Italian army, but felt I had to report it to the Italian CO. He took a serious view of the allegation and asked me what I felt should be done. I suggested that Capt. Gonzi and I investigated further and this was agreed. We went out at midnight on four mornings running to the bridge uniting the two countries over the Maritza and Tunja rivers, and stayed until dawn, but saw nothing.

I told Gonzi that the governor would not have made such accusations without good evidence, so he said he would make some internal enquiries, and came back with the information that when we had been seen going out, a telephone call would be made to the Bulgarian side asking about the weather which was the signal not to move any goods that night. We thus decided to spread the word that we had found nothing and were giving up, but went to bed early, rising at 03:00hrs and going separately to meet under the first arch of the bridge. By about 5 we had heard nothing and were about to give up again, when we heard the rumble of lorries [the word 'limbers' is used in the text], approaching the bridge. Gonzi suggested that I should move along to the next arch, whilst he would stop the convoy. I was to cover him; he felt that his men would not fire on an officer whom they knew, but might on a stranger. This worked well; two Italian soldiers crossed the bridge on horseback and blew a whistle which was the signal for the lorries to cross over. When they reached the spot where Gonzi was, he emerged and ordered them to stop; I also emerged from my hiding-place and covered him which also stopped them from turning back. He then got into the first lorry and gave them orders to proceed to the place which they had been going to. I got into the rear one. We drove on to a certain house, the gates opened for us into a large court, and then closed. I caught the man who had opened the gates and asked him who the goods were for; he replied that he did not know. "Why did you open the gates then?" I asked. I could get no further, so blew my whistle and called in the local Turkish police, explaining the situation to them.

In the meantime, Gonzi was making a roll-call of his Italians and found that there were 2 officers, 6 senior N.C.O's and about 20 men implicated who were all put under arrest, with him calling for further guards. I later reported back to the Italian colonel who confirmed that all the detainees had been sent back to Italy for trial. I also called on the local Turkish governor who told me that under his law, I was entitled to 50% of the sale value of the confiscated goods. I advised him that I was only doing my duty and refused any payment. On reporting the incident to my own

G.H.Q., I received the only reprimand I had during my time there. I was told not to waste my time preventing the smuggling of cheese from Bulgaria, as these goods helped in price control.

Quite soon after, a Mr Grancharoff called on me. He was a man I knew as the local manager of the Oriental Railways [? Orient Express], and I liked him. He asked if we could speak confidentially, so we moved into my drawing-room. "Well", he said, "you have ruined me, for the cheese which you confiscated was partly mine. My partners and I are willing to pay 200frs. in odd denominations now and 200 on future occasions, if you do not to take an active part in stopping future deliveries of contraband." I thought about the letter from HQ. which was telling me to do exactly what my friend was asking, but I knew that if I had accepted, he would have thought he had bought me. So I replied that I was not to be bought. I never saw him again, and so far as I could tell, the smuggling seemed to have stopped.

The work in Adrinople was not exacting. I visited the other posts at intervals, and decided that my brother Freddie in Rodosto [he would have been only 21, b. 1897] should be better relieved by a more senior officer.

I also had to visit a small town called Keshan at the request of the Armenian Orthodox Bishop in Constantinople, who informed me that some Armenian Christian girls were being held there in Turkish houses against their wishes, and that they should be returned to their proper homes. Before going there, I investigated the matter and learned that there was a single case of a Christian girl in the town; she was married to a Turk called Ismail.

I set off in an *araba* [a horse-drawn vehicle], as the roads were not safe for a car, with a driver and a batman; we were both armed, as the area was [still] full of deserters stopping vehicles and demanding money and food. It was mid-winter and very cold. The governor-general of Adrinople had given me a letter for the *vali* or mayor of the Keshan area, instructing him to obey my orders, and had also sent orders to two *jardirma* [*gendarmarie*] posts on the route to have fresh horses ready for us when we reached their positions. The journey took some 11 hours and we arrived very tired after dark, being escorted to our lodgings by some local gendarmes; a meal was ready for us, but I was surprised that the local mayor had not called on us as he should have done.

In the morning, I sent my batman to this local mayor to tell him that I was expecting him to call. He took his time and arrived about two hours later. I reprimanded him on his lack of courtesy, but he just smiled as if to say that he was not frightened of me, or of what his boss in Adrinople might try to do. I then informed him that I had come to see a Christian girl who was married to a certain Ismail, and that she had to be returned to Constantinople. He replied that he would not allow such a thing to happen, so I pointed out that I had the final decision in this case, and as such, my decision, not his would settle the matter and that I wanted to see the lady; difficulties were put in my way, but I insisted on seeing her, so I was eventually taken to Ismail's house, and after more discussions with his mother, was taken upstairs to see her. She had obviously just been put to bed with all her clothes on, and on asking her for her name, to my surprise said in broken English that she could not speak to me there. I therefore told her mother-in law that I could not carry out my duties in that house, and that the girl had to be brought to my lodgings. This created more trouble and I had to be very firm giving a direct order that the girl had to be brought to me. This took place later in the evening, possibly to allow a large crowd to accompany her shouting anti-Christian slogans, and when we were in the house, some stones were thrown at the windows.

Her story was that she originally came from an Eastern province of Turkey, but when the Kurds started to massacre Christians – mostly Armenians – she was sheltered by the lady who was now her mother-in-law. She remained hidden in the house for over a year, and when the son came home on leave from his army service, they fell in love and got married. The husband had to go back to his unit following his leave, but was discharged as unfit, later on. She also fell ill, but even though there was much deprivation in the area, she was always given the best food available. "My mother-in-law, before retiring for the night always insists on my saying my Christian prayers, and look, I still wear a cross around my throat. Do you want me to leave these people who love me, and send me to the bishop in Constantinople who cannot care for me and where I know no-one?"

I took a quick decision and called in the mother-in-law, kissing her hand and saying to her that I was proud to meet such a good woman – take your child back, and may the same God of Christians and Moslems bless you and your family. I accompanied them to the door where the crowd were ready for a hostile demonstration, but the lady told them of my verdict and what had happened and the mood changed. I was supposed to return to Adrinople the next day, but as we got ready to leave, we were stopped by a large crowd who insisted we stopped for the day and had a meal with the whole village in thanks for this evidence of British justice. Course followed course and speeches were made, all organised by the local Moslem *muezzin*. I was forced to say a few appropriate words. On my return to Adrinople, I reported that no Christian women were found in Keshan.

I often had to meet the French troops who held the right bank of the Maritza river. Their area was known as Western Thrace, and the head of their mission was a nasty old man, General Charpie. Whenever a matter of litigation arose between our areas, he would try to 'pull-rank' on me stating that as he was a general whereas I was only a captain, his decisions should prevail. I would reply that as respective Governors of Eastern and Western Thrace, we had equal rank, and our own personal military rank did not matter. I did ask G.H.Q to give me a local rank of half-colonel – without the pay if necessary – but they felt that the existing situation did not need changing.

The local Turkish military commander was General Jaffer Tayar, a real gentleman – we became good friends. We had a sort of understanding that when we were talking of matters not subject to military protocol, he would remove his *kalpak* or fur hat. One day, whilst visiting him on a military matter at his 1st Army HQ.'s, we heard fire bells, and found that a fire had started in a wooden building near his barracks. There was an old 'four-a-side' pump available, but the water tank was empty, and the men were running about throwing water from their buckets onto the fire, which was little use. I asked the general to take charge, and then organised the men to form a human chain and fill the tank, and to wait till it was full before using the pump. I realised that the only way to stop the fire from spreading further, was to stop it by the only brick-built house in the street. This meant we had to sacrifice the wooden house next to it. I got men to grapple with the timbers and pull it down after removing all the contents. I checked it before pulling it down and found a copy of the Koran had been left, so salvaged that, telling the owner that he should be ashamed of himself, leaving the holy book to be burnt. The fire did stop by the brick house, and only 11 houses were destroyed, whereas if it had jumped over that house, a real disaster might have occurred.

The next day, the local papers were full of praise for the adaptability of the British Officer who had saved the city from a major calamity. I had a visit from a man whom I did not recognise – he told me he was the owner of the house which we had pulled down, and he thanked me for saving all his goods and chattels, giving me as a present, the Koran which I had saved.

A few weeks later, I was at the station to see who was coming and going on the mainline train [to and from Constantinople], and saw a British major embark with two horses and many cases. I went up to him to enquire who he was, and he informed me that he was Major Harenc [sic], and that he was to take over from me. This came as a shock, as I had been there for about two years, and had heard nothing from G.H.Q. as to being moved. He too was embarrassed about this, but I said that I could not hand over without being told so by Constantinople. We had lunch together, and he asked if I would remain with him. I was not keen on suddenly becoming No.2 after so long in charge, but he said I could remain where I was and he had no intention of interfering in my work. Apparently, I had asked for a senior officer so many times, that G.H.Q. had decided to send him there. I told him that I did not mind handing the whole job to him, but was not prepared to act as his assistant. He said that as he had been keen to learn Turkish, he had been sent here, so once I had confirmation of his position, we continued as before with him taking no part in the everyday routines.

However, a few days later we were to become involved in a joint exercise with the French, when my friend General Tayar called on me, advising that we were now under open arrest. I laughed at this, but apparently he had received orders from one Mustafa Kemal Pasha who had started a revolution in Anatolia, that we were to be placed under arrest. I had never heard of this man before, but he was apparently the head of this movement [the 'Young Turks', Nationalists or 'Kemalists'.] I said that I would have to get instructions from my own HQ.'s in Constantinople, but he said that the lines had been cut, so this would not be possible. I suggested to Major Harenc that we turned the tables on the general locking him up, whilst we took our cars over to the French, and sent a wire via their system, but he did not agree to this action. I then asked the General if we could send a message to the French, but he did not agree with this either, suggesting that he would ask the French to wire us. We could remain in our house, as the major came to lodge with me. The Italians had long left the area.

The next day, Major Jeanbat, my liason officer with the French called and we asked him to get a message to our HQ.'s via his wireless [sic] which he agreed to do. The following day he reappeared and we thought he had a message for us, but he told us that his colonel wanted to know if they should march into the city and relieve us – we did not feel we had the authority for such a serious step. In total we sent three wires to HQ. asking for instructions, but the only reply was one asking if we wanted further rations[!]. We had been confined to the house for 9 days when I asked for the Turkish general to call back personally to find some way of ending this impasse. It was agreed that we should 'escape' by night, to the French lines. This we did after destroying all our papers, only taking that which we could carry in the two cars General Tayar allowed us to take. We arrived at the French lines at about 10pm telling the French that we had 'escaped' as agreed with the Turks. The French reported our arrival to our G.H.Q., who replied quite quickly that we should come back to Constantinople by train. This was easier said than done as much of the line had been damaged by Turkish troops. Following repairs we took an armoured train east and although expecting trouble on the way, arrived safely.

Major Harenc and I went to HQ.'s to report the whole history of the last few days, and we were given a few days rest and leave. I was then told to report to the censor's department; the work consisted mainly of checking newspaper reports. We had to assist at a morning conference where a daily report was handed out by a senior officer, and we had to see that nothing more than that which had been passed was allowed to be sent out. Our shift was from 8pm to midnight, after which we used to go for a drink to a place called the *Rose Noire*, where the servers were all Russian ladies [?]. I gave up going there when a certain Olga became too attentive.

POSTING TO IZMIT
In between the 'Loyalists' and the 'Kemalists'
The 'Montague Bates Force'

I was soon called back to G.H.Q. and told that I would be sent to Izmit [a port on the Asiatic side of the Sea of Marmara,] as chief Intelligence Officer to the 'Montague Bates Force'. I was told that Brigadier Bates was a difficult man and that I was to report back, direct to the Chief of Staff, as to any irregularities which I came across. I did not like the sound of this at all. On the train from Haydar Pasha [the main station for Constantinople on the Asiatic side; carriages going on to Europe used to be loaded onto barges and taken across to Sirkeji, the main-line station for Europe, and vice-versa], I met a Major Euler who was going to the same place, as the new Staff Major to Monty. I confided to him what I had been told about the colonel and he said that he had been instructed the same way!

On arrival at Izmit station, we asked the R.T.O. [Railway Transport Officer] where we could find the force HQ.'s, but he said he had never heard of it, and we had to ask the way to them from the Turkish authorities. We were directed back to the station, and found the Brigadier in a goods wagon in a siding which he had transformed into an office. I was ushered in and before I could say anything, the Brigadier began to abuse us suggesting that I was not much good to him as an Intelligence Officer if I could not find the way to his office, and by asking the Turks, I had given away his location. We tried to defend ourselves, but he got so angry that he banged his desk and upset the ink bottle, the ink pouring all over his papers. While trying to help to clear up the mess, he shouted "Get out!", so we took advantage [of it] to get away from this madman.

I booked into a small hotel in the town, and the following morning went back to the R.T.O. asking for a return voucher to Constantinople. I took this back to the Brigadier and asked him to sign it as obviously we could not work together, so it would be better if he had someone else on his staff. He stated that he would decide whether I stayed or left, to which I agreed. We then discussed how I should go about my work, and reached some sort of agreement that I would not keep to regular hours, as my brief was, by definition as an Intelligence Officer, one which would need flexibility. We agreed to try it for a week to see how we got on. After a week, I took my railway voucher back in for signature ready for my return to Constantinople, but he tore it up. We had begun to understand each other. I never saw him again after we disbanded, but had great respect for him and wished that I might have had the honour of serving under him again.

My work increased to such an extent that I had to move into a large house. There were six I.O.'s [Intelligence Officers,] and I chose the Christian part of the town feeling that any visitors or agents would be less likely to be observed there. These mostly came after dark and I had three entrances to the house so that they could come and go by different ways. At other times, we met outside the town, often through go-betweens. Our force consisted of an Infantry Brigade, that is, four battalions, but with RASC, RAOC and RAMC and howitzers and field guns for the gunners. We also had at least four destroyers in the bay, and sometimes two or three larger ships.

Our troops held a perimeter around the town and at first it was quite peaceful, but my agents began telling me that small forces of Kemalists had started to operate in the vicinity and were forcing villagers to billet and feed them. G.H.Q. then decided to start a force of Circassians who would be under our orders for technical purposes but would be commanded by their own officers. We would pay them a certain sum per day and they would have to provide themselves with horses, food etc. we giving them only arms and ammunition. They were a fine lot of men and brave fighters, but as the Kemalists got to know of this force they started to raid Circassian villages beyond our perimeter, mostly on the right bank of the river Sakaria.

The Circassians retaliated by raiding purely Turkish villages and thus created tension between us and the so-far peaceful Turkish villages.

[Circassia was an area in Caucasia. The region fell to Russia in the 1860's, and many of the tribes were forced to leave for the Ottoman Empire where they settled in various places, keeping themselves largely independent. When Lawrence of Arabia was captured by the Turks, he explained his blue eyes and fair complexion by claiming to be a Circassian. Their modern area is known as Chechnya nowadays].

The Brigadier suggested that we should show the flag in this area and we decided to go to as far as Kandra on the Black Sea, [my atlas shows a village/town named Kandira just a few miles inland from the Black Sea coast]. Our force was two battalions, one British and one Indian, with an advance guard of Circassian cavalry and we also had two howitzers. We had sent out word that we were out on a friendly exercise to the town, but were sniped upon from the beginning, so I told my Circassians to try to capture these snipers, and they rode on whilst I rode back to ask the Brigadier for further instructions. We camped for the night where we found good water and then the Circassians reported that the firing had come from a certain village, so we sent a message that we would shell this area giving them time to evacuate it, so that no-one would be injured or killed.

On our way to Kandra we found nothing but empty villages and even in Kandra itself there were just old people with children, all the male population having fled to the hills. We managed to procure some supplies making sure we paid for them, and began our march back. On the way we found the villages full of white sheets flying from the mosques as the villagers realised that we had no intention of attacking those who did not attack us. However, we did have to watch our flanks carefully and the Circassians complained that they had not been allowed to kill 'the enemy', but on this I was very firm – they could only capture those carrying arms. We did search some villages, only finding a few muzzle-loaders used by the villages for hunting, but against my advice, these were confiscated too.

The Kemalists now began to get more active, and we had to

take more serious measures against them. We were often fired upon from a hill to the north of the town and we had to hold it at night. Wire was placed around this 'sugar-loaf' hill, and a company was marched there an hour before sunset to remain there until an hour after sunrise. This was a dangerous place with two officers killed and two others wounded. I seemed to have a charmed life as I had to run bigger risks than any of them.

The political situation had become worse with the French and Italians courting the Kemalists, and the Greeks landing in Asia Minor [at Izmir, on the Mediterranean, not Izmit,] we were now the enemy. The Greeks advanced as far as the southern shore of the Gulf of Izmit and this naturally created tension with the locals. I suggested that a 'freezone' should be established. This was agreed and I took a launch to meet a local headman called Zeboglu Hassan. He was a fine and honest man, and one I felt I could rely on. I explained to him that I wanted to create an area of about 11 villages into which none of the fighting forces would be allowed to enter; neither the Greeks, but also not the Kemalists. He felt he had to consult with them, and later I was pleased to hear that it was agreed. The area provided much produce for the garrison, the area and even Constantinople itself, with boats taking vegetables and fruit there by boat.

Hassan often came to our garrison to report on progress and one day invited me to spend the day at his main village. This I accepted but said that I would go as a friend without arms, not as a soldier – this was agreed and I was met at the pier by a large group of villagers and entertained to lunch. When stating that I had to get back, Hassan said that he had told the launch which had brought me to return the next day. I was angry at this but had to put up with it. I was treated to an even bigger meal in the evening and slept very well, feeling grateful for the generous reception which I had been given.

This situation remained peaceful for some time, but soon Hassan complained to me that the Greeks kept raiding his area. I tried to reason with them pointing out how the current truce suited them, for if these villages became hostile, it would go against them, but only had an insulting reply, so I released Hassan from his promise and they sided with the Kemalists.

The 'loyal' government in Constantinople then decided to take the attack to the Kemalists and sent some troops to Izmit. General Bates felt this was a mistake and told them so, but they said that they only wanted access to the port and would march through the town camping, outside our perimeter. They landed with a great flourish of trumpets, parading a flag which had been given to them by the sultan himself. I had to see them through the town and they camped outside the perimeter as agreed. Needless to say they were an awful nuisance, as we had to remain friendly but neutral. They kept asking for items which we were not allowed to give them. They requisitioned all the local ovens to make bread leaving none for the local population, likewise vegetables, leaving us short as well. Eventually they decided to attack but were back on our lines soon after with the Kemalist's shells also reaching our own lines. The next day another sortie, which also quickly fell back in disorder. We reported this to G.H.Q. who must have contacted the Ministry of War as orders came for them to retire through our lines. We insisted that they handed their weapons to us before entering, and this order they seemed very happy to comply with. This was the end of the 'loyal' army which was supposed to clear Turkey of the Kemalist danger.

The Kemalists became more numerous and confident following this retreat and their shelling became a nuisance, so I was asked to go and parley with them. I went out alone carrying a white flag on a stick, but once it became dark, this was little use. The Turkish sentries heard me coming and began to fire, so I had to crawl along a ditch and shout to them that I wanted to speak to an officer. I heard people approaching, so put up my flag again shouting that I was a British officer wanting to get in touch with their commander, confirming that I was alone. Two men came forward pinning my arms and shouting that they had got me. An officer appeared and again I told him that I had been sent by my Commander-in-Chief to give a message to their local leader. They did not believe this and took me further inland where there was a more senior officer who said that I would have to give the message to him.

I replied that as an officer, he would know that if I had orders to speak to their local chief, this is what I needed to do. I was kept for a long time whilst they tried to get someone via their telephone link. At last I was called into another tent and given the instrument to talk. I asked who was speaking and was told it was General Izmet [sic – this man was Ismet Pasha, or Ismet Inonu who became the President of Turkey following the death of Kemal Ataturk in 1938.] I passed on my message saying that we were neutral in his conflict with the forces of the sultan, explaining how we had disarmed those troops who had passed back through our lines on their way back to Constantinople. He then promised that the firing would cease and I asked him that I be allowed to be escorted back to our own lines, and this was agreed after I had been blindfolded again and taken back to a different part of our lines where I was nearly shot by our own troops as those at that point knew nothing of my night's expedition.

I reported back to 'Monty' and asked him to inform HQ.'s, but he generously asked me to do so myself in order to get any thanks which might be forthcoming. I spoke to General Harrington and he seemed pleased at the success of my mission. [My father was awarded an MC for this operation – see details on p.154].

As the Kemalists were again becoming more aggressive due to the constant incursions by the Greeks, we had to repel several attacks on our long perimeter and we had an order to make a sortie towards the Sakaria river and clear up the area up to and including the town of Ada Pazar. The country was not as hilly as the road to Kandra but we were still harassed by snipers. I was the first to be fired on almost before starting; the head of the column was clear of the town but the tail was not when a bullet took my hat off. The Circassians with us dispersed in a sort of screen around me but two were killed and several wounded. We arrived at Ada Pazar to learn that the main body of Kemalists had crossed the river Sakaria, so our Brigadier asked me to send the Circassians over to keep in touch with them and report back.

In the morning we were just about to cross over, having heard that the Circassians had practically trapped the Kemalists when a 'plane came over dropping a message from G.H.Q. ordering us to return to Izmit at once. I passed the word over to the Circassians who were really angry, and we started to march back not knowing what to expect back at base camp. On arrival at Izmit we found our

HQ. occupied by a large staff of officers with General Ironside in charge. Our CO. and the new general had heated words and when Brigadier Bates came out of the meeting, he was white with rage, said good-bye and having collected his belongings left us with hardly a word.

We found out later that he had been reprimanded for having tried to cross the Sakaria river 'against orders'. We also gathered that whilst we had been away his safe had been opened by the new staff in order to try to find evidence against him. 'Monty' was sent home soon after arriving back in Constantinople and we heard that he had resigned his commission following this dirty trick on him. He was a great loss to the army, for though not liked by many, was a first-class soldier.

On one occasion the Greeks made a raid on a village just north of the town from which some snipers were operating. They returned with hostages, but killed most of them just outside the town. I reported this, and a mission was sent to investigate. Three senior officers were sent; one each British, French and Italian. The British and French officers began to question witnesses, but the Italian refused to see anyone saying that he would weigh-up the evidence taken by the others and give his decision based on those reports. I do not think that anything was ever done. It is true that the Greeks killed the hostages, but every time the Greeks had sentries on the perimeter, these were shot.

I assisted at a court martial ordered by a Greek general after the murder of one of his despatch riders. The man had been killed just outside a Turkish village and the murderer had been seen running back into the village. From the description given, the Greeks went into the village to arrest a certain man called Ali who lived next to the village *hoja* [local Moslem priest.] This man pretended he did not know any 'Ali', even though the man's mother gave evidence that her son lived next to this *hoja*. With no evidence, nothing could be done, and so the crime went unpunished.

Rumours began to circulate that the Greeks would be leaving the Izmit area; I went to see General Gargalides who said there was no such intention. There was to be a plebiscite in Greece to decide whether the country was to remain a kingdom, or become a republic. This Archipelago Division was very largely Venezelist, so the result locally was a foregone conclusion. Every officer and soldier had to cast his vote in an empty kerosene [paraffin] tin which was sealed when full and taken to the port from where they would be taken by the destroyer '*Lion*' [whether British or Greek is not clear] to Athens to be opened and counted. You can imagine our surprise when we heard that the result was a large Royalist victory, and even our division had voted 85% for the King.

The true story was told to me several years later by the man in whose house the voting tins had been kept. Barges came ashore from the '*Lion*' with similar urns to the ones with the voting papers. The correct urns were taken on board, but then thrown overboard when at sea, and the new ones substituted. This is how elections are carried out in these parts.

After this election, many of the officers were replaced by Royalist ones. However, I learned from a Greek officer, a Venezelist, but not a militant one that the division would be leaving soon, although this was still denied by General Gargalides. I felt that I had to get the truth and the only way seemed to be that I had to tap the Greek wires. I had two men listening day and night to conversations and orders, and soon had enough evidence to feel that I could report to G.H.Q. I sent three reports and one night General Harrington himself rang me to ask why I was giving him this information when he had just been told the opposite by a senior Greek liaison officer. I told him that I was sorry to disagree with him, but they would be leaving in three day's time. He asked me how I came about my information, but I said I could not tell him over the phone.

The next day I had a telegram which said that HMS *Seref* had been sent for me, and would take me to HMS *King George* where I was to report to C.i.C. on board, and that I was not to report my conversation of yesterday to anyone. The *Seref* took me to the larger ship and I went at once to the C.i.C. who asked me how I had obtained these 'mad' reports about a Greek withdrawal. He told me that he wanted me to tell this news to three generals who had been called on board for a meeting, without telling them how I had obtained this information. I gave him the names of the ships by which most of the equipment had left the port and also the names of ships expected to take the residue of the Greek troops.

I pointed out that with the absence of Greek troops, the Turks would follow and would not be kindly disposed towards the local villagers; I was told to mention this to the generals as well.

At the meeting was my old adversary, the French General Charpie [see p. 127], a General Monbelli and the Greek liaison officer; Charpie was not pleased to see me again. I was told to tell them what I knew. General Charpie asked me how I dared to contradict the Greek general who still insisted that there were no plans for a withdrawal, but that he would check with his HQ. He left the room to make contact, and came back later – I had never seen such a change in a man. He admitted that he had been misled, and that it was a fact that their troops were being withdrawn, and that quite soon. I said that my information suggested that it was to happen in two days' time and that we should make plans to evacuate those Jewish and Christian people who might want to leave Izmit. The difficulty of shipping then came into question as no ships were available to cope with a possibly large exodus. I was told to return to Izmit and inform the heads of the local communities of the facts.

I was promised a destroyer to pick up my own staff, but no one else. I put in a plea for the Circassians, and I got an assurance that a special boat would be sent for them as well, but that they would have to leave their horses and most of their belongings. One of their chiefs asked me not to let his bed fall into Turkish hands, and on enquiring why, he admitted that the uprights were of solid gold. We did not have time to save even this treasure.

On informing the facts to the heads of the local communities, panic set in and they all sent representatives to me to ask for my help, which I was not able to give. The next day, small craft of every description arrived to take away the refugees. It was a pitiful sight seeing families going on board with just the one bundle of possessions which they were allowed to take. The quayside became littered with goods and furniture which had to be left behind. The evacuation fully took up the two days which we had, with flares at night helping people load the boats to take people away, mostly to Constantinople, but some only as far as Darija.

The departure of the final Greek troops was fixed at 11, and at 9, people were still embarking when some Turkish villagers came to tell me that some Greeks were massacring their people. I jumped into my car and saw some really horrible sights, and was told that some departing Greeks had set fire to certain parts of the town. This was more important, and I left the mutilated bodies and tried to help to deal with the fire. I then rushed back to my billet where my staff were getting restless, to tell them to go to the pier where they would find a picket boat to take them to the destroyer, then send it back for me. I went back into the town and was assured by the Turks that I would be safe if I stayed there. I found the Roman Catholic priest, who told me he was staying to look after those poor people who had asked for his protection. [This shows what a cosmopolitan town Izmit was at the time].

Whilst there, some friendly Turks told me that the Kemalists were already entering the town; so I ran down the hill to the pier and was fired on as I crossed the railway line. Luckily the picket-boat had returned and we pushed off; I was glad to be under the White Ensign. We were fired at again, and saw some Greek boats overloaded with booty which probably never got to safety with their cargo, although we advised a Greek destroyer, by signal, that these boats were in the bay.

THE 'KEMALISTS' TAKE OVER
Allied withdrawal from Turkey

Back in Constantinople, I was received by General Harrington who praised me for my work in Izmit, giving me a few days leave, saying he would call on me later for further duties, and I was suddenly called-upon to go to Broussa [Brusa] to replace a certain Major Wilson whose reports always gave glowing accounts of the Greek army. I took the ferry to Mudania [Mudanya] and was met by Wilson's driver in his car, but the major had left that morning. I put up at the pension where the major had stayed and when asking where his office was, learnt to my surprise that it was in the Greek HQ. The next day, I called there, but as I did not have a proper letter from our G.H.Q. appointing me as his replacement, they would not accept me, and I did not get any satisfaction from Constantinople.

I thus spent my time trying to find if I could trace any former colleagues from Izmit in the city, and eventually found just the man I wanted. He was a Venezelist who was fed up being amongst so many Royalists. He gave me information which I felt was so biased that I did not report it, especially as it would have arrived after [and contradicted] the glowing accounts of the Greeks which had come from Major Wilson. I confirmed however, some of the more detailed facts, like the park of brand-new Leyland lorries always shown to visitors, of which only about six had any engines in them. To get a visual confirmation of this, I had to rope in an American girl-friend of mine [?] who was to be used as bait to a Greek officer. The three of us went for a riding trip, and I managed to fall just before we started, telling them to move on and I would catch them up. I asked the sentry on duty to get a bandage for my 'wound', and whilst he was away, lifted the bonnet of a truck and found it had no engine, confirming my report.

Other Venezelist officers told me that morale was very low, as the supply officers were getting rich selling supplies to civilians, and the Royalists making things difficult for those who did not think their way.

I sent two strong reports to HQ. by special courier, but not having a safe in my office, did not dare keep copies. They got fed up with my reports, as these clashed with the pro-Greek ones they had been used to getting, so I was recalled and sent to Gebze, [back in the Gulf of Izmit.] My section as Advanced Intelligence Officer started there and went as far as Yarimca. I had an engine [?] at my disposal, as well as a drezine [sic] with a Turk as a driver. After a while I reckoned I would do better in Hereke, and moved there, half-way inside my domain. There was a company of Indian troops in this village, and I was able to lodge in a chalet built for Emperor William II [?]. Life was pleasant, but monotonous. I used to go about getting bits of information here and there, and was told once that agent 113 would be passing through without proper papers, and I was to allow him to continue [?]. I knew this old man quite well, and pretended to have missed him, but was surprised to find him jumping off the train as it moved away. He stayed with his boy-friend in Gebze, and was eventually replaced by the Kemalist whom he was supposed to spy upon. [?]

Istanbul [sic] was very short of vegetables, and we were short of grain, so I suggested to General Harrington that I should try to set up a barter arrangement with the Kemalists, and he gave me *carte blanche* to proceed. I took my drexine [sic- spelt differently here] with my driver, both of us unarmed, and with a white flag strapped to the vehicle, proceeded into no-man's land. We were very soon stopped and ordered to put our hands up, which we did. I tried to explain that I was a British officer, that my driver was a Turk and that I wanted to speak to one of their officers, but they said that they had orders to kill anyone from our side – they had never heard of a white flag. I tried to humour them, saying it would be more fun for them if they killed us in their camp rather than in this desolate spot, and luckily they agreed with this, so we proceeded with the car, very slowly to their camp with two sentries behind us with their guns in our backs. When we arrived at their camp, they shouted to their comrades that they had brought in two enemies to kill. Luckily a young officer appeared, and I was never so glad to see a Turkish officer as I was then. Unfortunately, his captain had gone on to Izmit for a conference, so I asked if he could contact him, but this took some time. I noticed that they did not seem to be well-provisioned as the coffee they offered us had practically no sugar. He also suggested that if I came again, a bottle of *raki* would be welcome.

It took a long time to get through to anyone in authority, but eventually he gave permission for us to come to Izmit with an escort, and we met a colonel there who luckily was in charge of supplies; he heard what I had to say and agreed to pass on the proposal to higher authority for approval. We agreed to meet again in a week, and I suggested that if the reply was favourable, he should bring with him someone who knew exactly what they wanted from us. When we met again the following week, there were about 30 of them, with very few military. We had prepared a written document stating what we wanted, and a list of non-military goods was set up, with prices as ruling in the Constantinople markets. A train would leave Haydar Pasha with goods for them; at Yarimca one of their crews would take it over and return the next day with our supplies, and the crews would change over again. There would be three trains a week with no passengers. We had two more meetings to settle detail before the plan started, and it was a blessing to both sides.

One of my Turkish agents informed me one day that arms were being unloaded at Darija, and were being hidden in the Greek church in the town. I did not like the priest there, as I had heard that he had seduced his own daughters after his wife died [Greek Orthodox priests are allowed to marry, and live in their community]. His third daughter had come to me for help when he had tried the same thing with her. I went out with night field-glasses for three nights on a hill overlooking Darija Bay, and did see a Greek ship arrive with large cases being unloaded and taken to the church. The next day, I raided the church with some troops and found more than a thousand rifles hidden there and in the priest's house; these were to be used for a coup against Constantinople which was to be led by my old friend 'Colonel' Yoannou. I gave details of other places where arms were supposed to have been hidden, but do not know if any more were found.

When the main Turkish advance took place, the Greeks were pushed back in as many days as the months it had taken to get where they were. General Harrington asked me why I had not advised him of this likelihood, and I had to tell him that I had done just that when I had been in Brusa, but that no-one had acted, feeling that the new man's opinion was so different to that of Major Wilson, that it had been ignored. Luckily the officer who had received my reports agreed that they had come through, but as they had seemed so ridiculous, he had binned them. That officer got his bowler hat the same day, [presumably meaning that he was sent back to civilian life].

The Kemalists began to move towards Constantinople, and life became very hectic. My agents stopped feeding me information fearing that these Kemalists would not appreciate their co-operation with the British. I thus had to tap into a line which we discovered underground. The messages went through at about two in the morning, and were not even coded as they had no idea we were listening-in to them. Our post was above Scutari [Uskudar] with a busting [?] station and manned by men who knew Turkish well, so everything was written down.

One day I was asked to provide a good meal for 10 people on a train which would proceed to Izmit to collect and take on to Constantinople, the mission which was to go on to Lausanne to discuss peace terms. I was to collect a man from an intermediate station – *Kizil Toprak* [red earth,] who was named as the head of the Turkish Red Crescent [Islamic Red Cross,] but in fact was a senior Kemalist who was very anti-British, and made us wait, so that we arrived late in Izmit. I was prevented from leaving the station, so I had to send a messenger to the waiting delegation to tell them that the meal we had prepared was ready and waiting for them. A message came back with a Turkish major, that Ismet Pasha [the officer my father had had dealings with earlier,] felt that he had to eat with the loyal citizens of Izmit, but would I join them. This I did, much to the anger of my disagreeable friend. I told the major to collect some of his friends and avail himself of the banquet we had prepared on the train. The meal I had was much inferior! The speeches after the meal were very unfriendly, and I felt most uncomfortable at what was being said against us. Ismet Pasha later apologised to me saying it was as well to let these people let off steam, to which I agreed.

On the way back, I tried to be in the same compartment as Ismet Pasha, but my nasty friend tried to ensure that I did not enter 'the presence'. However, I managed to get in when this man was not watching, offered Ismet Pasha some cigars which he accepted with good grace, and had a few non-political words with him reminding him of the earlier incident in the hills above Izmit when we had spoken on the telephone and then we discussed non-political matters until the train arrived at Constantinople. He went on to stay with friends in the city; I reported to General Harrington and was kept for dinner with him and his charming wife.

The question of the day was whether the Turks would accept the terms imposed on them during the Lausanne Conference. However, following negotiations agreement was reached, but not with the blessing of the Greeks.

On St Patrick's Day, the Irish Guards gave their last parade in their barracks square, and I was invited to it, but going in civvies with no pass, I was not allowed in, much to my frustration. Later there was a Trooping of the Colours parade in Taksim Square which was very imposing with thousands watching. Later we had to assist at a sadder ceremony with the hauling-down of the Union Jack at the Dolma Bache landing stage, and the raising of the Turkish flag whilst we presented arms. After that, the Commander-in-Chief left the parade ground amid shouts of 'yuha' which was an insult, used as a term to move cattle along. The Commander however, took this as 'hurrah', and wired home to this effect, very much to the amusement of the locals.

Here I must add some personal details. In 1919, my previous employers, the Imperial Ottoman Bank in London, who had kept paying my salary right through the war, asked me when I would be returning. I raised this with G.H.Q. who advised that I could not be spared, and the bank continued to pay me. In 1921, they again wrote and said that I was losing all chances of promotion, and that I should try to return to Britain soon. I went to see General Harrington with this letter, and pointed out that I was not a regular,

I had had no promotion, and that as my post was only temporary, it was not fair to be refused my chance to return to my old job. He seemed rather hurt by my insistence, and said it would be better if I resigned from the bank, as they had better things in hand for me. I replied that as he was a soldier, I felt safe under his command, but once the military left, the next man in charge might not feel the same way about me. He agreed that he would be moving on, but that the current High Commissioner would remain and be made ambassador, and that I would be working under him.

He then rang Sir Horace Rumbold, the current High Commissioner, and arranged for me to see him personally to have the situation explained to me. Sir Horace seemed astonished that I was uncertain as to my future, and said that seeing as I had been sent in by General Harrington, he would let me into a secret, and called a secretary for my file to be brought in. He then folded over a certain page, and showed me two typed lines which said "proposed post, Governor of Eastern Thrace or sub-governor of Smyrna [Izmir,] salary £1,200". This went to my head, and with muttered words of thanks I left his office. I then wrote to the bank telling them that I still could not be released, so the only honest thing to do was to resign, and I offered to pay back the money they had paid me. They replied with a charming letter, refusing any repayments and even let me have my life insurance premiums back. I had thus burnt my boats so far as that lovely institution was concerned, but was looking forward to better times ahead.

However, once the Greeks were beaten, I could not see how the proposed post in Thrace would apply, so again called on Sir Horace, who told me not to worry as he had given me his promise. I was then given a 'temporary' job under a Major with a pay of £75 pm, which was more than my salary with the bank, but one day he called me in and said that I had been axed, adding that the 'Geddes Axe' [this was a belt-tightening exercise following excessive wartime expenditure] had affected me. I immediately asked to see Sir Horace again and reminded him of his promise – "Have you anything in writing?" was his response. I was so shocked at his change of attitude, that I left the room without speaking. This hurt, not so much for the loss of the prestigious posting, but because my own side had let me down. The Major said he would get me three months' pay as an exceptional item, so I found myself adrift with some £200 in the bank and £225 to come. I was the idiot who had believed in their word.

Once the troops left, the British were not at all popular with the Turks who are a deeply patriotic nation. We had occupied their country, and had treated them as inferiors, using minority groups as interpreters and advisers. We had placed in every official office, a notice on which was printed "Remember Kut", [Allied forces took this town in Mesopotamia from the Turks in Sept. 1915 but were besieged and it was recaptured by the Turks in April 1916. There were allegations of cruelty to the captured British and Indian forces, and this notice was used as a warning not to fraternise with the Turks.] The minorities took full advantage of this, playing-up to it. They only had to say that they were Greek, Armenian or Jewish, and had been badly treated by the Turks, to receive aid, and many of them had made money from this situation.

The police [? policing] of the area had been divided into three areas. The British had Pera, the most important, the French had the old city which was the main Turkish area, and the Italians the Asiatic side. The local officer in charge was Lt. Col. Maxwell; I had known him as a major when working in the Struma area with the 82nd Brigade, and he had been a hard-working and responsible superior, but now just seemed to feel his work had been done and he could relax, leaving too many decisions to his Greek interpreters who took full advantage of the situation.

He seemed not to realise that he was being subtly bribed by being given items which he admired when invited to certain houses, and then granting special favours "as they are such nice people". When he left, his photo was printed in the papers with a list of the items he had received cross-referenced to the number of each case. This was a pity as he had been a good and efficient officer.

The Italians seemed to understand the mood of the locals best. They had a mixed population on the Asiatic side, and they managed to keep all sides happy although perhaps too fond of the ladies, but of course were not the only ones with those inclinations. The French had mostly black troops in the area. When the question of a plebiscite arose as to who should govern the whole city, the Italians let it be known that they would give Italian nationality to all who applied for it. When this did not have the desired result, they then offered Lts.5 to all applicants. This had serious results, as many Armenians took up the offer and began to travel abroad with these Italian passports. Once all the Allies left, all these passports were cancelled, leaving those abroad with no status, and not able to return. The Turks then confiscated all their property in the country; this was not quite fair, but there was nothing these unfortunates could do.

GENERAL MUSINGS ON THE POLITICAL SITUATION

[The earlier pages are typed and numbered 1-45, but then, in the binder appear eight pages typed on a different paper, and dated. The earlier pages are not dated. I will treat these new ones as a separate 'chapter', as it is not clear how they might fit-in with the earlier entries].

21.10.1922. Arrived in Uzunkopru [near Izmir on the Mediterranean] to work on the mission as Political Officer under Colonel Tweedie; there is also a Colonel Halliard with a large white beard and a clever Italian Commander Neyrone. They seem to work well together.

23.10. Went to Chakmak by car. The village has been burned completely by Greek refugees on the way out. Found a dead Turk and a Greek body, badly mutilated. The Turks would not accept that a Greek had been killed.

24.10. Went to Eskikoy. Refugees still pouring in; our men and the Greeks are trying to help, but can do little. Some of the poorer ones are carrying large loads, the better-off ones seem to have left everything behind, as they were not able to obtain transport; some of them hope to return and have left goods with Turkish neighbours.

25.10. Uzunkopru has about 2,000 Turkish houses, 1,000 Greek, and 60 Jewish ones. The majority of the Greek population has left, leaving only a few merchants who are trying to sell their goods to the remaining Jews at absurd prices. Turks and gypsies are looting the Greek houses, even taking doors and windows. Went on to

Salefkoy, a large Greek village of some 800 houses which was famous for its wine. The villagers are not able to take this away with them and are drinking it with the result that they are causing all the trouble in the area. The Greek army is requisitioning far more than it needs, but we are not able to interfere. Met General Gargalides whom I had met before in Bandirma when I had been sent to help the Manissa division in Izmit: to work under us, so they have lost all the territory which they had gained with so much hard work. Wires arrive asking us to stop the Greeks looting Turkish property, but as usual, these orders come too late as most of the looting has already taken place.

27.10. Back to Eskikoy. Saw nothing but chaos. Col. Tweedie seems reluctant to act and will not give orders to his unit. It seems that a cereal commission is to be formed – how clever of G.H.Q. to think of this now that every barn has been looted. There are seven military commissions in place; one railway and a liaison one. We now will have this cereal one and their work will add up to nil.

30.10. The last of the Greek Army has gone through. The army arrived with flags flying and drums beating and now they are leaving looking very sorry for themselves. The Turks are waiting until they have gone to loot what they will leave behind. What a ghastly sight is a defeated army; the officer did not even try to make their men look like soldiers; they all felt the shame of defeat.

1.11. The Greek sub-prefect wrote [in] saying that as he was unable to carry out his duties, he was resigning. Of course we did not accept his resignation, but on the other hand we should face facts. The colonel refuses to do this; all I can get out of him when I suggest taking preventative action is "my men will soon stop any trouble if any starts". We had received orders from HQ to register all houses evacuated by the Greeks and had started to do so. I was in favour of letting the Turks enter houses which had been evacuated, feeling that an occupied house is better protected than an empty one, and we would note that the house of – say – a Papdopulo was temporarily occupied by an Ali. This, our colonel would not allow, and actually gave orders for any Turks who had entered Greek houses to be ejected. Capt. Moss was put in charge of this unpleasant work. Today Col. Emery turned up and saw what was happening; he was furious and called on Col. Tweedie saying that this would have to stop.

I really do try to treat both sides alike, and I am accused as being pro-Turk by some and pro-Greek by others.

2.11. Back to Salefkoy which is now a mass of ruins. I had gone alone with a driver. On the road, came across a group of Turks with rifles which I confiscated.

3.11. Went to Tivorno; a pretty village which had been used by Greek refugees. It is in ruins. It was destroyed by the villagers of Pavlokoy who are Pomaks [?]. The roof of the church had fallen in and the holy books were torn and had been trampled upon.

4.11. Went to Kavakjikoy. This village was reported as having been burnt by the departing Greeks: in fact, only three houses were burnt, but the Italian officer only took photographs of these three burnt houses. Such is the work of the 'impartial' commission.

7.11. The colonel is convinced that this show is simply run for the benefit on the Constantinople staff; and that they would recommend the complete evacuation of our troops and let the Turks and Greeks fight it out. What he is thinking is that he wants to get out and retire to Gibraltar, where his wife is living.

10.11. Had two day's leave in Constantinople. It was a nice change, but the situation there is not so pleasant. The Nationalists have taken over the Government. The last of the grand Viziers has gone. How Abdul Hamid [?] must laugh in his grave. The Sultan was asked to go, but refused. This is our last chance and we should stand for the Caliphate, thus rehabilitating ourselves in the eyes of the Islam world. I wrote to Col. Gribbon with my opinions, as I felt this was my duty. I wonder if they will jump at the chance or will they use this precious moment to organise a boxing tournament?

12.11. A quiet day following violent demonstrations in the town which were repressed by our soldiers.

13.11. Had a meeting with the colonel and Major Ewal [sic,] the 2.i/c. The colonel feels that he could settle the whole situation with his machine guns and trench mortars, and that if asked, volunteers in Britain would come out and fight the Turks again. I tried to suggest that if the people of Britain had been asked in 1914 if they wanted to fight the Germans, the answer would have been No!

He summed up his ignorance of the situation by saying that a year ago he did not even know where Thrace was!

15.11. A Colonel Lucas has come to replace Johnson at Keshan. He was liaison officer to Nider [?], but now he goes as 'Political Officer'. He has two cars, one typewriter, a groom, a batman, a secretary and two orderlies. Why he should be going there when the Gordons are leaving today for Rodosto [Tekirdag] beats us all.

18.11. The arrival of Shakir Bey [?] His convoy consisted of some 800 people with 400 gendarmes in four companies. He is a tall man with very sharp features. He was employed by Haji Adil in Adrinople during the war: not a good recommendation. I do not think him a clever man, but he has with him as his head of the Political Bureau Ghalib Bahtiar who is the moving spirit. Bahtiar is head of the Thracian committee, a clever man with cruel eyes and expression.

[There now follows a few pages where my father comments on the political situation and on the Lausanne Conference being held on 20th November. I do not feel that they are particularly interesting or relevant, but if a Turkish publisher became interested in these offerings, these contents might be worth further editing for inclusion].

AFTERWORD
TO HENRY NEWBOLT LYSTER'S
DIARIES

My father decided to stay in Constantinople, and applied to various UK companies for agencies eventually becoming an agent for Roneo and John Tann's Safes, but he was not a businessman.

He was married to my mother, Virginie Josephine Catherine Vitalis, a daughter of a well-known local Italian family in 1924, by one Bishop Roncalli, then the Apostolic Delegate to the Greek Orthodox Church, whose centre was still in the city. This man went on, of course, to become Pope John Paul XXIII.

My brother, Alfred Anthony (aka. Alan) Lyster was born in the city in 1925, but in 1932 the whole family was expelled from Turkey, with 72 hours to leave the country or be taken to court and tried for drug smuggling. My brother, then seven, recalls three Turkish civilians with two soldiers bursting into the apartment and going straight to a sofa, under which he used to keep his box of toy soldiers, and pulling out some bags of a substance. These had obviously been 'planted'.

We both feel that our father was still trying to gain intelligence; that the 'agencies' were purely a front and that the local consulate advised him to leave rather than face the embarrassment of a show-trial, as much later, my brother met a man (in Khartoum in the 1950s) who recognising Alan's surname, asked whether he was any relation to one Henry Lyster. On being advised of the relationship, this man hinted that he had been told to award our father certain commercial agencies to enable him to remain in the city.

I was born in London in 1937, but my mother and I returned to Istanbul in 1947, as my father – once more in the military – had been seconded to the RAF, as they, with De Havilland, were trying to sell Vampire (military) jets to the Turkish Air Force, and a Turkish-speaking liaison officer was required.

Following demobilisation in 1948, he returned to Istanbul obtaining work at the British Consulate in the city. In 1953 he was moved to the old Colonial Office in Cyprus as part of 'Special Branch' to help deal with the troubles there with 'Enosis, (Union with Greece)' and 'Eoka'. He finished work in 1960 when Cyprus became independent, and retired to Istanbul where he became active with the local British Legion being awarded the MBE for his services to them. He died in 1980 (aged 92), and is interred in the Vitalis family vault in the Catholic cemetery in the Harbiye area of the city.

He was awarded the Greek Silver Cross of George II in 1919; the citation is hand-written in French and is difficult to decipher.

He was also awarded the MC in 1922 – the citation (No. 0737/9405) reads Lt. (T/Capt) Henry Newbolt Lyster, 3rd Bn. London Rg. Att. [attached] Intell. Corps.

> "For gallantry and devotion to duty on 14th June 1920, during the Ismid [sic] operations against the Nationalist Forces when despatched under heavy rifle and machine-gun fire with a message to the Anti-Nationalists [Kemalists], which he succeeded in delivering. His intelligence work throughout the operations was invaluable".

What I find surprising is the amount of responsibility my father had when still just a lieutenant, if T[emporary]/Capt. as British Military Representative in Eastern Thrace. The French had appointed a general to be their equivalent officer in Western Thrace.

INDEX TO THE DIARIES OF MRS MARIE LYSTER

INDEX TO THE DIARIES OF CAPTAIN HENRY NEWBOLT LYSTER